Data Management in the Cloud

Challenges and Opportunities

Synthesis Lectures on Data Management

Editor
M. Tamer Özsu, *University of Waterloo*

Synthesis Lectures on Data Management is edited by Tamer Özsu of the University of Waterloo. The series will publish 50- to 125-page publications on topics pertaining to data management. The scope will largely follow the purview of premier information and computer science conferences, such as ACM SIGMOD, VLDB, ICDE, PODS, ICDT, and ACM KDD. Potential topics include, but not are limited to: query languages, database system architectures, transaction management, data warehousing, XML and databases, data stream systems, wide scale data distribution, multimedia data management, data mining, and related subjects.

Data Management in the Cloud: Challenges and Opportunities
Divyakant Agrawal, Sudipto Das, and Amr El Abbadi
2012

Semantics Empowered Web 3.0: Managing Enterprise, Social, Sensor, and Cloud Based Data Services for Advanced Applications
Amit Sheth and Krishnaprasad Thirunarayan
2012

Foundations of Data Quality Management
Wenfei Fan and Floris Geerts
2012

Incomplete Data and Data Dependencies in Relational Databases
Sergio Greco, Cristian Molinaro, and Francesca Spezzano
2012

Business Processes: A Database Perspective
Daniel Deutch and Tova Milo
2012

Data Protection from Insider Threats
Elisa Bertino
2012

Data Management in the Cloud: Challenges and Opportunities

Divyakant Agrawal, Sudipto Das, and Amr El Abbadi

ISBN: 978-3-031-00767-5   paperback
ISBN: 978-3-031-01895-4   ebook

DOI 10.1007/978-3-031-01895-4

A Publication in the Springer series
SYNTHESIS LECTURES ON DATA MANAGEMENT

Lecture #32
Series Editor: M. Tamer Özsu, *University of Waterloo*
Series ISSN
Synthesis Lectures on Data Management
Print 2153-5418   Electronic 2153-5426

Data Management in the Cloud

Challenges and Opportunities

Divyakant Agrawal
University of California, Santa Barbara

Sudipto Das
Microsoft Research

Amr El Abbadi
University of California, Santa Barbara

SYNTHESIS LECTURES ON DATA MANAGEMENT #32

ABSTRACT

Cloud computing has emerged as a successful paradigm of service-oriented computing and has revolutionized the way computing infrastructure is used. This success has seen a proliferation in the number of applications that are being deployed in various cloud platforms. There has also been an increase in the scale of the data generated as well as consumed by such applications. Scalable database management systems form a critical part of the cloud infrastructure. The attempt to address the challenges posed by the management of big data has led to a plethora of systems. This book aims to clarify some of the important concepts in the design space of scalable data management in cloud computing infrastructures. Some of the questions that this book aims to answer are: the appropriate systems for a specific set of application requirements, the research challenges in data management for the cloud, and what is novel in the cloud for database researchers? We also aim to address one basic question: whether cloud computing poses new challenges in scalable data management or it is just a reincarnation of old problems? We provide a comprehensive background study of state-of-the-art systems for scalable data management and analysis. We also identify important aspects in the design of different systems and the applicability and scope of these systems. A thorough understanding of current solutions and a precise characterization of the design space are essential for clearing the "cloudy skies of data management" and ensuring the success of DBMSs in the cloud, thus emulating the success enjoyed by relational databases in traditional enterprise settings.

KEYWORDS

Cloud computing, database management systems, scalability, elasticity, self-manageability, multitenancy, transactions, consistency

To Shubra.
– Divyakant Agrawal

To Pamela Bhattacharya, my friend of all times and my constant source of
inspiration.
– Sudipto Das

To Janet Head.
– Amr El Abbadi

Contents

Preface

Big data and cloud computing are two heavily used terms in the research literature and popular media. As we stepped into this era of cloud computing and the associated data deluge, one question continually asked was: "What are the new challenges in cloud data management?" This book evolved as a result of our quest to answer this question and educate ourselves with a deeper understanding of this problem-space. The journey toward this book started with an initial survey paper summarizing the major design principles that allowed key-value stores, such as Google's Bigtable, Amazon's Dynamo, and Yahoo!'s PNUTS, to achieve unprecedented scale by spanning thousands of servers within a data center and potentially to multiple data centers in different parts of the world. As this area caught the attention of more researchers in academia and industry alike, the field advanced beyond key-value stores into scalable data stores supporting richer guarantees such as transactions, or schema beyond the simple key-value model. As such, it was time for us to extend our brief survey of three systems into a three hour-long tutorial presented at VLDB 2010 in Singapore and then at EDBT 2011 in Uppsala, Sweden. Numerous presentations of related material have followed since these tutorials and our understanding of this space also evolved with time. Many more systems were also proposed in the meanwhile. This book summarizes much of our learning from over the course of these years and many interesting discussions that have resulted from our presentations.

Similar to the classical divide between transaction processing and data analysis systems in the traditional data management landscape, cloud data management also has a similar divide. On one hand, are systems targeted mainly at data storage and for serving Internet-facing applications. These systems resemble classical transaction processing systems, although with many different characteristics. On the other, hand are data analysis systems, similar to data warehouses, that analyze massive amounts of data to glean knowledge and intelligence from them. As enterprises aggressively collect data about their users and combine data collected from various different sources, MapReduce-based systems, such as Hadoop and its ecosystem, have democratized this space of data analysis and warehousing. With tens of open-source offering and potentially hundreds of research papers in related areas, the data analysis space in the cloud is a thriving research area. This area will see continued proliferation given the quest for enterprises to obtain competitive advantages by obtaining insights from their data repositories.

Our study, analysis, and surveys have focused on the first class of systems, namely the data management and storage systems. Therefore, this book will only focus on such systems. This book will delve into the challenges in designing these update-intensive systems that must provide quick response to queries/updates that access small portions of the database. In this class, we further subdivide our study into two classes of systems. In the first class, the challenge is in scaling the systems to serve large applications with thousands of concurrent requests and hundreds of gigabytes to terabytes of frequently accessed data. The second class comprises the scenario where a cloud service provider must efficiently serve hundreds of thousands of applications each with a small footprint in terms of query load and resource requirements.

Divyakant Agrawal, Sudipto Das, and Amr El Abbadi
December 2012

Acknowledgments

Our journey toward this book started a few years back with a desire to better understand the design space of cloud data management. The result is a manifestation of our evolving understanding of this space. This evolution was made possible with help from many people around us, too numerous to name. However, we would like to take this opportunity to thank some of those who played an important role in its synthesis.

First, we would like to thank our series editor M. Tamer Özsu who gave us the opportunity to write this book and provided us with continuous support and feedback throughout the process. He meticulously read earlier drafts and made copious comments and corrections that considerably improved the document. Diane Cerra provided us the necessary administrative support as the Executive Editor with our publisher, Morgan & Claypool. Without this help and support from Tamer and Diane, this book would not have materialized.

Much of the material in this book has been presented in various forms at different venues across the world. During the course of these presentations, we have received feedback from many attendees that have directly or indirectly improved our presentations and often provided a different perspective. We are extremely thankful to all who have provided this generous feedback. We have also benefited from the numerous discussions with Shyam Anthony, Philip Bernstein, Selcuk Candan, Aaron Elmore, Wen-syan Li, Klaus Schauser, and Junichi Tatemura. We would like to thank them all. We (Agrawal and El Abbadi) would also like to acknowledge the contributions of all our graduate students from our graduate courses (CMPSC 271 and CMPSC 274) from 2008–2012.

Finally, we would like to thank our respective families for bearing with us for the countless hours that have gone into preparing this book and related material. Without their constant support and understanding, this book would not have seen the light of the day.

Divyakant Agrawal, Sudipto Das, and Amr El Abbadi
December 2012

CHAPTER 1

Introduction

Current technology trends have resulted in an increase in the number of user applications, services, and data that are hosted in large-scale data centers, metaphorically referred to as the *cloud*. Cloud computing has commoditized computing infrastructure similar to many other utilities in our life and has considerably reduced the infrastructure barrier between an innovative application and its deployment to reach a large number of users dispersed geographically in any part of the world. Prior to the advent of cloud, market validation of a new application with a vast user base amounted to huge upfront investments on computing infrastructures to make the application available. With *pay-as-you-go* pricing in cloud infrastructure and *elasticity*, i.e., dynamically provisioning or removal of servers depending on the load, many of these infrastructure risks have been transferred to the cloud infrastructure providers, thus allowing an application or service to reach a global user community and impact many users. Consider the examples of applications such as Foursquare, Instagram, Pinterest, and many more which are being accessed by millions of users worldwide; such large-scale deployments are made possible by cloud computing infrastructures.

While the cloud platforms simplify application deployment, the service providers now face unprecedented technological and research challenges to develop server-centric application platforms that are available to a virtually unlimited number of users 24/7 over the Internet. Experiences gained in the last decade from some of the technology leaders that provide services over the Internet (e.g., Google, Amazon, and Ebay) indicate that application infrastructures in the cloud context should be highly *reliable*, *available*, and *scalable*. Reliability is a key requirement to ensure continuous access to a service. Similarly, availability is the percentage of times that a given system will be functioning as required. The scalability requirement indicates the system's ability to either handle growing amounts of work in a graceful manner or its ability to improve throughput when additional resources (typically hardware) are added. Scalability has, in fact emerged both as a critical requirement as well as a fundamental challenge in the context of cloud computing.

In general, a computing system whose performance improves after adding hardware, proportionally to the capacity added, is said to be a scalable system. There are typically two ways in which a system can scale by adding hardware resources. The first approach is when the system scales *vertically* and is referred to as *scale-up*. To scale vertically (or to scale-up) means to add resources to a single server, or replace a server with one with more resources, typically involving more processors, memory, and I/O capacity in a single server. Vertical scaling up is quite effective in providing more resources to the existing set of operating systems and application modules, but does require the replacement of hardware components. Furthermore, beyond a certain scale, a linear increase in a server's capacity results in super-linear increase in costs, thus considerably increasing the infrastructure costs. The alternative approach of scaling a system is by adding hardware resources *horizontally* referred to as *scale-out*. To scale horizontally (or scale-out) means to seamlessly add more servers, and distribute the load. New servers can be incrementally added to the system, thus allowing the infrastructure costs to increase (almost) linearly, thus making it more economically feasible to build large capacity computing infrastructures. However, such horizontal scaling requires efficient software methodologies to seamlessly manage these distributed systems.

As server prices drop and performance demand continues to increase, low-cost "commodity" systems can be used to build large computing infrastructures to deploy high-performance applications such as web search and other web-based services. Hundreds of commodity servers may be configured in a cluster to obtain aggregate computing power which often exceeds that of many powerful supercomputers. This model has been further fueled by the availability of high performance interconnects. The scale-out model also creates an increased demand for shared data storage with high I/O performance especially where processing of large amounts of data is required. In addition to these hardware and infrastructure trends, *virtualization* has provided an elegant solution to managing and sharing such large infrastructures even at the granularity of sharing single servers. This scale-out paradigm is fundamental to today's large-scale data centers, which form the essential infrastructure for cloud computing. Technology leaders such as Google, Amazon, and Microsoft have demonstrated that data centers provide unprecedented economies-of-scale since multiple applications can share a common infrastructure. All three companies have taken this notion of *sharing* beyond their internal applications and provide frameworks such as Amazon Web Services (AWS), Google AppEngine, and Microsoft Azure for hosting third-party applications in their respective data center infrastructures, called *public cloud*.

Figure 1.1 presents a simplified view of the software stack of web-based applications deployed in a cloud infrastructure. The clients of the applications connect to the application (or *service*) over the Internet. The interface to the application is typically through an application gateway or a load balancer that routes the requests to the appropriate servers in the web and application server tier. The web tier processes the requests and encapsulates the application logic. For fast access, frequently accessed data items are typically stored on a set of servers that comprise the caching tier. Such application caches are typically distributed and are explicitly managed by the application tier. The application's persistent data are stored on one or more database servers that comprise the database tier. Data stored in the *database management systems* (DBMSs) typically comprise the *ground truth*, i.e., data that the application relies on for its normal operation. Most applications deployed in these large cloud infrastructures are data driven. Data and therefore DBMSs are an integral technology component in the overall cloud software stack. Since the DBMS is such a critical component of the stack, data is often replicated (shown in broken lines in the figure). Such replication provides high availability in the event of one DBMS server failing. Another challenge is to handle the growing scale of data and the number of requests. In this book, we will focus on these challenges in designing the database tier of the cloud software stack.

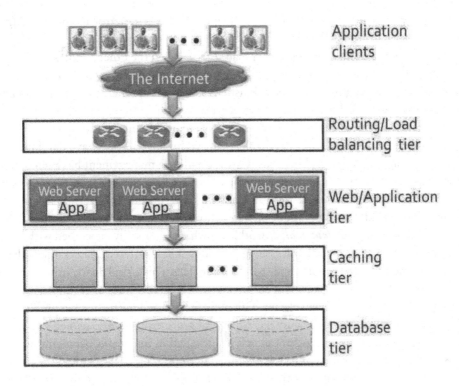

Figure 1.1: A simplified view of the software stack of a typical web-based application deployed in a cloud infrastructure.

The reason for the proliferation of DBMSs in the cloud computing space is due to the success of DBMSs, and in particular *relational DBMSs* (RDBMSs), have had in meeting the data modeling, storage, retrieval, and querying requirements of a wide variety of applications. The key ingredients to this success are due to many features DBMSs offer: overall functionality (modeling diverse types of applications using the relational model which is intuitive and relatively simple), consistency (dealing with concurrent workloads without worrying about data becoming out-of-sync), performance (both high-throughput, low-latency and more than 25 years of engineering), and reliability (ensuring safety and persistence of data in the presence of different types of failures).

In spite of this success, during the past decade there has been a growing concern that DBMSs and RDBMSs are not *cloud-friendly*. This is because, unlike other technology components for cloud service such as the web-servers and application servers (which can easily scale from a few machines to hundreds or even thousands of machines), DBMSs cannot be scaled very easily. In fact, current DBMS technology fails to provide adequate tools and guidance if an existing database deployment needs to scale-out from a few machines to a large number of machines.

The requirement of making web-based applications *scalable* in cloud computing platforms arises primarily to support virtually unlimited numbers of end-users. Scalability of a system is a static property in that it only provides the guarantee that a system can scale to large numbers of servers or user requests. That is, scalability does not specify whether the system's scale can be dynamically adapted to fluctuations in user load. *Elasticity*, on the other hand, is a dynamic property which allows the system to dynamically scale-up by adding more servers or scale-down by removing servers without incurring any downtime. Elasticity is a crucial property of a system to benefit from the elasticity of the underlying cloud infrastructures.

Driven by need to scale-out to thousands of servers, being elastic, spanning multiple geographical regions, and being always available, many technology leaders have developed proprietary data management technologies. Historically, the task of data management has been broadly divided into two classes with very different requirements. The first class comprises *on-line transaction processing* (OLTP) or in general *data serving* workloads which is concerned with the execution of typically short and simple read/write operations or transactions. The second class comprises *decision support systems* (DSS) or in general *data analysis* workloads which is typically concerned with long duration, read only, and complex analytical processing operations. These different classes of workload pose different requirements on the systems and there has also been a historical divide in system architectures tuned for each class of workloads. Not surprisingly, two parallel lines of technologies have evolved targeting these different workload classes. This book focuses on how the former problem, i.e., OLTP, has been approached in the cloud context. Analytical processing has also gained significant traction related to cloud-based data management and has resulted in important paradigms and systems. In particular, the *MapReduce* paradigm was proposed within Google [Dean and Ghemawat, 2004] as a programming model, which is particularly suitable for large analytical problems on large data sets executed on clusters of computers. The paradigm, in its simplest form, partitions a large input data set and *maps* each partition to a different server. Each such server solves the original problem on the smaller subset, and passes the result to a *reducer*, who collects all the results from the various mappers, combines its inputs to produce the final output. Evangelized by Google and popularized by its open source counterpart Hadoop [Apache Hadoop], the MapReduce paradigm is one of the most notable new technologies in the cloud era. While the debate on MapReduce versus RDBMSs tuned for data analysis continues [Dean and Ghemawat, 2010, Stonebraker et al., 2010] and a vibrant research activity advances the state-of-the-art in MapReduce and Hadoop-based analytical platforms for the cloud, our focus for the rest of this book will be on data-serving systems in the context of cloud.

An early trend in scalable data-serving systems designed for the cloud were a class of systems called the *key-value stores*. Systems such as Bigtable [Chang et al., 2006], Dynamo [DeCandia et al., 2007], and PNUTS [Cooper et al., 2008] set the trend and were closely followed by a slew of open-source systems that either replicated the design of these in-house systems or were inspired by these. The main distinction of key-value stores when compared to RDBMSs is that in traditional RDBMSs, all data within a database is treated as a "whole" and it is the responsibility of the DBMS to guarantee the consistency of the entire data. However, in key-value stores, this relationship is completely severed into keys and their associated values where each key-value pair is treated an independent unit of data or information. The atomicity and consistency of application and user accesses are guaranteed only at a single-key level. This fine-grained consistency allowed the key-value stores to horizontally partition the database, freely moved data from one machine to the other, distribute data across thousands of servers while obviating heavy-weight distributed synchronization, and continue serving user requests while certain fragments of the database might be unavailable as a result of failures. Furthermore, key-value stores were designed to be elastic while traditional DBMSs were in general intended for an enterprise infrastructure that is statically provisioned and the primary goal was to realize the highest level of performance for a given hardware and server infrastructure.

All the initial in-house systems were custom designed with well-specified requirements to cater to certain application characteristics. For instance, Bigtable was designed to support building and serving the index structure that powered the Google search engine. Similarly, the shopping cart of Amazon.com's e-commerce website was the primary motivation for Dynamo and Yahoo!'s social properties drove the design of PNUTS. As a result, even though these systems are grouped in the broad category of key-value stores, each system makes some crucial design choices that differentiate them. Later in this book, we analyze each of these systems in detail to understand these design choices and their associated trade-offs. However, the key properties of scalability, elasticity, and high availability made these systems highly popular within their respective applications and in the broader community through their open source alternatives such as HBase, Cassandra, Voldemort, and many more. This resulted in widespread adoption of these systems which was heralded in popular media as the NoSQL movement [NoSQL]. While atomicity and consistency at the granularity of single key-value pairs was adequate in the applications that motivated the design of such key-value stores, in many other application scenarios this access-pattern is not enough. In such cases, the responsibility to ensure atomicity and consistency of multiple data entities is on the application developers. This results in the duplication of *multi-entity synchronization mechanisms* many times across different application stacks. The realization of providing access guarantees beyond single entities was widely discussed in developer blogs [Obasanjo, 2009] and elsewhere [Agrawal et al., 2010, Dean, 2010, Hamilton, 2010].

In general, the main challenge is the ability to support atomic access to multiple data fragments in the database while still ensuring efficient performance, scalability, and elasticity. Hence, it became clear that the classical notion of *transactions* [Eswaran et al., 1976, Gray, 1978] needed to be supported in the context of large data centers. Distributed transactions have been well studied [Özsu and Valduriez, 2011], however, the traditional and practical wisdom has been that they do not ensure high performance, and result in slowing down the entire system, especially in the presence of failures, which are common in large clusters of servers. This fundamental design trade-off and the various proposed design alternatives form the crux of the discussion in the subsequent chapters of this book. In particular, we analyze various systems and approaches either proposed as academic prototypes or as industrial-strength offerings. These approaches often exploit subtle properties and access patterns of the applications or restrict the functionality provided to the application layer. The challenge is to provide increased functionality, while not sacrificing performance, scalability, and elasticity of key-value stores. In fact, at this point in time, it can be argued that the success of cloud platforms seems to be critically contingent on at least making data management expressive, scalable, consistent, and elastic in a cloud setting.

While scaling the DBMSs to the requirements of a single large application with large numbers of concurrent users remains a challenge, many cloud platforms also face the challenge of serving large numbers of small applications that are deployed in such platforms. For instance, cloud platforms such as Microsoft Windows Azure, Google AppEngine, and Salesforce.com, serve hundreds of thousands of applications many of which have a small footprint in terms of data storage or the number of concurrent requests that must be served. A major challenge is to support these applications in a cost-effective manner. This has given rise to *multi-tenancy* where multiple tenants share a common set of resources and co-exist within the system. Multi-tenant databases are emerging as an important and critical component in the software stack of a cloud platform. These tenant databases typically are not that large, and hence, can reside exclusively in a single server. As a result, the entire functionality of a DBMS can be easily supported, namely, both SQL as well as transactions. However, the problem of elasticity, effective resource sharing among the tenants, and efficiently consolidating large numbers of small tenants are still quite significant. This has resulted in various approaches to *virtualization* in the database tier. The concept of virtualizing the hardware and system software has been predominantly proposed and used in sharing and managing large data center infrastructures. However, virtualization within the database to support and isolate multiple independent tenant databases has recently garnered significant interest both in the database research community as well as the commercial offerings. Toward the latter part of this book, we discuss the fundamental challenges in designing such elastic multi-tenant database systems.

Cloud computing and data management in large-scale data centers build on fundamental computer science research in both distributed systems and database management. In Chapter 2, we provide some basic background material in both distributed computing and databases, especially distributed databases. Many of the topics covered in Chapter 2 are fundamental and are needed to understand some of the advanced concepts discussed in later chapters. However, a reader familiar with the literature in these areas can skip to Chapter 3 which covers some of the early work in data management in a cloud setting, namely, key-value stores. In particular, we cover some of the basic trends and lessons learned from that experience, and highlight some particular systems. We then start our discussion on how to support atomic operations (transactions) in a cloud setting. In Chapter 4, we discuss some of the first attempts which concentrated on co-locating required data on a single site, which then could be accessed atomically on that site without resorting to complex distributed synchronization protocols. Chapter 5 then provides more general solutions where transactions are truly distributed and access data that is dispersed across multiple sites or even data centers. In Chapter 6, we discuss the topic of multi-tenancy and explore different approaches for supporting live migration in a cloud setting. Chapter 7 concludes with some lessons learned and directions for the future.

CHAPTER 2

Distributed Data Management

The foundations of cloud computing are based on many of the fundamental concepts, protocols and models developed over the years in Computer Science, and especially in distributed computing and distributed data management. In this chapter, we cover some of the basic background in distributed systems and data management, which forms the foundation of many cloud database systems. Our goal is to provide the reader with enough context to help understand some ideas used in latter chapters. The informed reader can skip the familiar parts. We also refer the reader to standard texts on distributed database systems [Gray and Reuter, 1992, Özsu and Valduriez, 2011, Weikum and Vossen, 2001] for additional details. This chapter starts with a coverage of the foundations of distributed systems in Section 2.1, which include the causal model of computation, time, and various logical clocks; distributed mutual exclusion and the notion of quorums; leader election; multicast protocols; and a discussion of consensus, Paxos, and the CAP Theorem. This is followed in Section 2.2 with an overview of Peer-to-Peer Systems, which have been extensively used to manage data in clustered data centers. In Section 2.3, we provide an overview of fundamental concurrency control and distributed recovery protocols in distributed database systems.

2.1 DISTRIBUTED SYSTEMS

We now provide a brief overview of some of the fundamental concepts that provide the underpinning of distributed systems, and that lay the foundations for many of the concepts and protocols used in cloud computing and data centers. The main abstraction of a distributed system is that it is a collection of independent computing processes or processors, often referred to as nodes, that communicate with each other through a communication network using message passing. This abstraction implies that the processes on nodes do not share any memory, have independent failure modes, and share no common clock. Nodes may fail by crashing, fail-stop, or even maliciously. The network may have link failures. In general, the system might suffer from partitioning failure, i.e., is divided into several sub-partitions, where nodes in a single partition can communicate with each other, but no communication occurs across partitions. Partitioning failures may occur due to both link as well as node failures, as in the case of a gateway failure.

Distributed systems are also classified into *synchronous* and *asynchronous* systems. In an *asynchronous* distributed system, no bounds are known on the times for message transmission, processor processing, or on local clock drifts. In a *synchronous* system, such bounds are known, and hence *timeout* can be used to detect failures, and when needed, act accordingly.

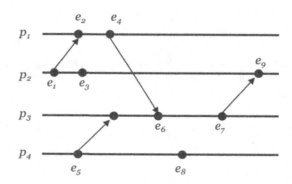

Figure 2.1: Events and messages

2.1.1   LOGICAL TIME AND LAMPORT CLOCKS

In his landmark paper in 1978, Lamport proposed a simple model for distributed systems [Lamport, 1978]. In this model, a process is modeled as a sequence of totally ordered *events*. Events are of three kinds: *local*, *send*, and *receive* events. A send event sends a message, which is received by a corresponding receive event. A local event can be a non-communication event, e.g., put or get in memory, multiply two matrices, etc. Figure 2.1 illustrates an example of a distributed system consisting of four processes: p_1, p_2, p_3, and p_4. Events e_2 and e_4 are executed on process p_1, events e_1, e_3, and e_9 are executed on process p_2, and so on. Event e_3 is a local event on process p_2, while event e_1 is a send event, and e_2 is the corresponding receive event.

An event *e happens before* event f, denoted $e \rightarrow f$ if

1. The same process executes e before f

2. e is $send(m)$ and f is $receive(m)$ where m is a message

3. There exists event g so that $e \rightarrow g$ and $g \rightarrow f$.

The happens before relationship captures the potential causal dependency between any two events. Furthermore, we say that two events e and f are *concurrent* if neither $e \rightarrow f$ nor $f \rightarrow e$. In Figure 2.1, event e_4 *happens-before* event e_6, while event e_3 is concurrent with both events e_2 and e_4.

The notion of time, and its relationship to events is critical for many distributed systems protocols. Often, real (or even approximately real) time clocks are not needed, rather, a notion of time that captures potential causality suffices. Lamport introduced a notion of logical clocks that do capture potential causal relationships between events. Namely, a *logical clock* assigns a value $clock(e)$ to each event, e, such that for any two events e and f:

- if $e \rightarrow f$ then $clock(e) < clock(f)$.

In order to implement such a logical clock, Lamport proposed assigning each process a clock counter. This counter must be incremented between any two events in the same process. Furthermore,

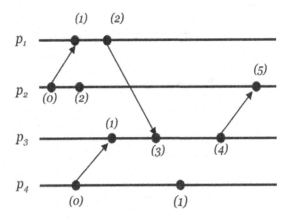

Figure 2.2: Lamport clocks.

each message carries the sender's clock value. When a message arrives at a destination, the local clock counter is set to the maximum of the local value and the message timestamp + 1. It is easy to show that this implementation satisfies the above logical clock condition.

In Figure 2.2, we use the same example of Figure 2.1, and assign logical times with all events in the system.

Since the *happens-before* relationship is a partial order, several events can be assigned the same logical time clock. In many protocols it is convenient to have unique values associated with events. In this case, and in order to break ties, time value is considered a pair $\langle t, p \rangle$, where t is the logical time given by the local clock counter, and p is the process identifier of the process where the event was executed. It is typical to assume that processes have associated with them unique totally ordered process-IDs. The process ids are used to break ties between events that share the same logical time.

2.1.2   VECTOR CLOCKS

Logical clocks capture potential causality, however, they do not imply causality, i.e., the logical clock condition is only a necessary condition, and not necessarily sufficient. A stronger clock condition would be one that requires for all events in the distributed system e and f:

- $e \rightarrow f$ if and only if $clock(e) < clock(f)$

This condition can be implemented by associating with each process i a vector V_i of length n, where n is the number of processes in the system. Each event is assigned the value of the local vector, when it is executed.

Each vector is initialized to 0, i.e., $V_i[j] = 0$ for $i, j = 1, \cdots N$. A process i increments its element of the vector in local vector before each event, $V_i[i] = V_i[i] + 1$. When process i sends a message, it piggy-backs the message with the local vector, V_i. When a process j receives a message,

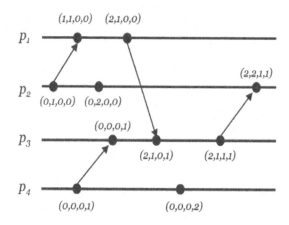

Figure 2.3: Vector clocks.

it compares the received vector and its local vector element by element and sets its local vector to the higher of two values, i.e., $V_j[i] = max(V_i[i], V_j[i])$ for all $i = 1, \cdots, N$.

Now for two vectors V and V', $V = V'$ iff $V[i] = V'[i]$ for all $i = 1 \cdots N$ and $V \leq V'$ iff $V[i] \leq V'[i]$ for $i = 1 \cdots N$. Note that $V < V'$ if there exists at least one j ($1 \leq j \leq N$) such that $V[j] < V'[j]$ and for all $i \neq j$, where $1 \leq i \leq N$, $V[i] \leq V'[i]$. For any two events $e, f, e \rightarrow f$ if and only if $V(e) < V(f)$, and two events are concurrent if neither $V(e) < V(f)$ nor $V(f) < V(e)$.

In Figure 2.3, we assign vector time values to all events in the example of Figure 2.1.

Although vector clocks exactly capture causality, their size is a function of the size of the network, which can be quite big, and every message must carry this additional vector.

2.1.3   MUTUAL EXCLUSION AND QUORUMS

Mutual exclusion is a basic concept that arises whenever concurrent processes access shared resources. It is a fundamental operation in operating systems, and is generalized to locking in databases. Mutual exclusion can be defined as follows: given a set of processes and a single resource, develop a protocol to ensure exclusive access to the resource by a single process at a time. Many solutions have been proposed, both for centralized as well as distributed systems. A simple centralized solution for the distributed mutual exclusion problem is to designate one process as the *coordinator*, and when a process needs to access the resource, it sends a *request* message to the coordinator. The coordinator maintains a *queue of pending requests*. When the coordinator receives a *request* message, it checks if the queue is empty, in which case it sends a *reply* message to the requesting client, who accesses the shared resource. Otherwise, the *request* message is appended to the queue. Once a process finishes its execution on the shared resource, it sends a *release* message to coordinator. On receipt of a release message, the coordinator removes that request from the queue, and checks queue for any pending

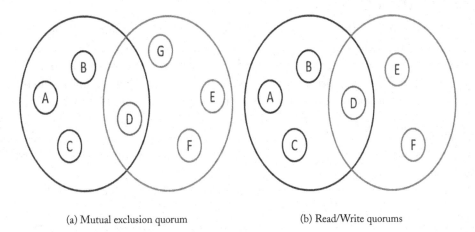

(a) Mutual exclusion quorum   (b) Read/Write quorums

Figure 2.4: Quorums.

requests. This protocol has been generalized to a distributed protocol, with no central coordinator by Lamport [1978], and optimized by many other researchers.

The straightforward generalization of this basic protocol requires the participation of *all* processes in the system. To overcome failures, the notion of *quorums* was proposed by Gifford [1979]. The crucial observation was that any two requests should have a common process to act as an arbitrator. Let process p_i (p_j) request permission from a set q_i (q_j), where q_i and q_j is a *quorum*, and can be a subset of all the processes in the system. Then the intersection of q_i and q_j must be non-empty. For example, a set which contains a *majority* of the processes in the system forms a quorum. Using quorums, instead of all the processes in the system, the basic protocol still works, however, it may suffer from deadlocks [Maekawa, 1985]. Figure 2.4(a) shows an example of a system with seven processes, any set of size 4 or more must intersect with any other set of size 4 or more, i.e., any two quorums, each containing a majority of sites must have a non-empty intersection.

In the context of databases, the notion of quorums was generalized as the standard operations are read and write, and read operations do not need mutual exclusion. Rather, multiple read operations can execute concurrently, but a write operation still needs exclusive access to the data item. Hence, two types of quorums were developed: *read quorums* and *write quorums*, where two write quorums must have a non-empty intersection, and a read and a write quorum must also have a non-empty intersection, but no read quorum intersection is mandated. Figure 2.4(b) shows an example of a system with six processes, where a write quorum is any set of size 4, and a read quorum is any set of size 3. Note that any read and write quorums must intersect, and any two write quorums must intersect. However, read quorums do not necessarily intersect, and hence multiple read operations can be executed concurrently.

2.1.4   LEADER ELECTION

Many distributed algorithms need one process to act as coordinator, and typically, it does not matter which process is actually chosen. This problem is often referred to as *leader election*, and the critical aspect is to ensure that a single unique coordinator is chosen. The protocols are fairly simple, and typically require that each process has a process-id, and all process-ids are unique and totally ordered. We illustrate the protocols using the representative *Bully Algorithm* [Garcia-Molina, 1982], which for simplicity assumes that communication is reliable. The key idea is to try and select the process with the highest process-id. Any process can initiate an election if it just recovered from a failure or if it suspects that the current coordinator has failed. Three types of messages are used: *election, ok*, and *I won*.

Processes can initiate elections simultaneously. An initiating process *p* sends *election* messages to all processes with higher IDs and awaits for *ok* messages. If no *ok* messages are received, *p* becomes the coordinator and sends *I won* to all processes with lower IDs. If it receives any *ok* messages, it drops out and waits for an *I won* message. If a process receives an *election* message, it returns an *ok* message and starts an election. If a process receives an *I won* message, then the sender is the coordinator. It is easy to argue the correctness of the Bully Algorithm. Election protocols have also been proposed that use a logical communication structure or overlay, such as a ring. Chang and Roberts [1979] proposed one such protocol that arranges the nodes in a logical ring where each process knows its neighbors, and the goal is again to select the process with highest ID as coordinator. A process starts an election if it just recovered or detects that the coordinator has failed. This process sends an *election* message to the closest downstream node that is alive by sequentially polling each successor until a live node is found. Each process that receives the *election* message tags its ID on the message, and passes it along the ring. Once the message reaches back to the initiator, it picks the node with highest ID and sends a special *coordinator* message along the ring, announcing it is the leader. Note that multiple elections can be executed concurrently.

2.1.5   GROUP COMMUNICATION THROUGH BROADCAST AND MULTICAST

When data are replicated among several nodes, updates need to be sent to *all* copies. A simple communication primitive is the *broadcast* or *multicast* operator. Typically, a broadcast sends the same message to all sites in the system, while a multicast restricts it to a subset. Without loss of generality, we will use the term *multicast* to refer to sending the message to a specific set of nodes. We now describe various primitives that have been proposed and have been used in different contexts in distributed systems as well as data centers.

FIFO or sender ordered multicast: Messages are delivered in the order they were sent (by any single sender)

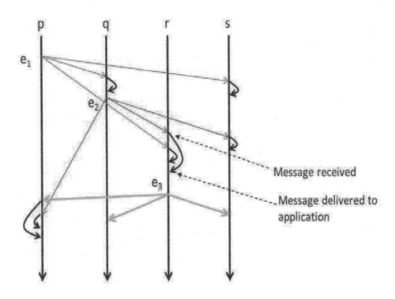

Figure 2.5: Causal ordering.

Causal order multicast: If two messages m_1 and m_2 are sent, such that the send event of m_1 happens
before the send event of m_2 then the delivery of m_1 must occur before the delivery of m_2 at
all common destinations.

Total order (or atomic) multicast: Messages are delivered in the same order at all recipients.

The main challenge when implementing these various multicast protocols is to develop a
method that ensures the ordering constraints. The underlying network is assumed to only support
point-to-point communication, and does not support any multicast primitive. Furthermore, we
distinguish between the *receipt* of a message through the network, and the actual *delivery* of the
message to the application layer. When a message is received, it is inserted in a queue, until the
ordering conditions are satisfied, and the message is ready for delivery. We now provide high-level
descriptions of some protocols that implement these primitives. Figure 2.5 shows an example of
three causally related broadcasts e_1, e_2, and e_3. If these broadcasts are causal broadcasts, then the
delivery of some messages must be delayed until the *causal order* condition is satisfied. So, for example,
although broadcast e_2 is received by process r before the receipt of broadcast e_1, since e_1 *happens
before* e_2, then the delivery of e_2 at r is delayed till after e_1 is received and delivered. Similarly, e_3 is
delivered at all processes after both e_1 and e_2 are delivered. As another example, consider Figure 2.6,
also with three broadcasts e_1, e_2, and e_3. Even though e_1 and e_2 are not causally related and are
broadcast from two different processes, p and q, if they are total order broadcasts, then all sites must
deliver them in the same order, irrespective of the order in which they are received. So, for example,

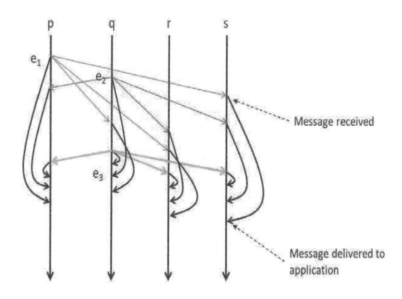

Figure 2.6: Total ordering.

although broadcast e_2 is received by process r before the receipt of broadcast e_1, and at process s the order is reversed, all sites must deliver the two broadcasts in the same order, e.g., all sites deliver e_2 before e_1. Note that even if the send operations are causally related, total order does not require the causal order to be observed—e.g., e_2 and e_3 are causally related, and even though e_2 *happens before* e_3, the delivery could be to have all processes deliver e_3 *before e_2*.

FIFO multicast are easily implemented using a simple TCP-like delivery protocol, i.e., using ordered message identifiers that are ordered by the sender, and each message waits until all previously ordered messages are received and delivered. If a message is found missing, the recipient can send to the sender requesting the missing message.

Causal multicast can be implemented by requiring each broadcast message to carry all causally preceding messages. Before delivery, the recipient ensures causality by delivering any missed causally preceding messages. However, the overhead of such a protocol is significant. Alternatively, the following protocol (used in ISIS [Birman, 1985]), uses vector clocks to delay the delivery of a message until all causally preceding messages are delivered. Each process maintains a vector clock, V, of size n, where n is the number of nodes in the system. Initially entries in V are set to 0. When a node i sends a new message m, the entry corresponding to node i is incremented by 1. Each message is piggy-backed with the local vector of the sender. When a node delivers a message, it updates its vector by replacing each entry by the maximum of its local value and that of the vector that arrived with the message. A node i delivers a message m with vector VT, if the entry corresponding to the sender in VT is exactly one more than the entry for the sender in the local vector at the receiver

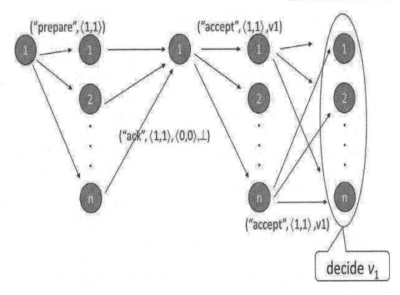

Figure 2.7: Rounds of Communication in the Paxos Protocol.

(i.e., this is the next message), and that all entries in the local vector are greater than or equal to the corresponding entries in VT, i.e., the receiver has received all causally preceding messages.

Total order multicasts can be implemented using a centralized approach, for example a fixed coordinator (used in Amoeba [Kaashoek et al., 1989]), or even a moving token [Défago et al., 2004]. Alternatively, a distributed protocol such as used in ISIS [Birman, 1985] has been proposed. In the ISIS distributed protocol, processes collectively agree on sequence numbers (or priority) in three rounds. The sender sends the message m with a unique identifier to all receivers. Receivers suggest priority (sequence number) and reply to sender with the proposed priority. The sender collects all proposed priorities; decides on the final priority (breaking ties with process ids), and re-sends the agreed final priority for message m. Receivers deliver message m according to the decided final priority.

2.1.6   THE CONSENSUS PROBLEM

Consensus is a fundamental distributed systems problem that involves several processes agreeing on a value in the presence of failure [Pease et al., 1980]. The problem is often posed in a context where communication is reliable, but sites may fail either by crashing or even maliciously, i.e., responding in ways that do not follow designated protocol or code. In general, the problem can be defined to involve a single coordinator, or *General*, which sends a binary value to $n - 1$ *participants* such that the following conditions are satisfied:

Agreement. All correct participants agree on same value.

Validity. If the general is correct, every participant agrees on the value the general has sent.

We start with two impossibility results. In an asynchronous system, Fischer et al. [1983, 1985] proved that consensus is *impossible* to solve if one process fails even by crashing and processes communicate by message passing. On the other hand, in a synchronous system with malicious failures, Dolev [1982] proved that *no* solution exists for a system with fewer than $3f + 1$ processes where f is the maximum number of faulty (malicious) processes.

Several protocols have been proposed to solve the consensus problem in synchronous and asynchronous systems. Synchronous systems specify an upper bound on the maximum number of failed malicious sites, i.e., one third. On the other hand, asynchronous systems may not guarantee termination. Recently, the Paxos protocol proposed by Lamport [1998, 2001] for asynchronous systems has gained much popularity. Abstractly, Paxos is a leader-based protocol where each process has an estimate of who the current leader is. When a process desires to achieve consensus on a value, it sends it to the current leader. The leader sequences the operation and launches a consensus algorithm to ensure agreement. In general, the protocol proceeds in two phases. In each phase the leader contacts a majority of sites, and in general, there may be multiple concurrent leaders. Ballots are used to distinguish among values proposed by different leaders. The two phases can be summarized as follows: Phase 1, or the prepare phase, where a node that believes it is the leader chooses a new unique ballot number, which is sent to all sites, and waits to learn the outcome of all smaller ballots from a majority of sites. Phase 2, or the accept phase, where the leader proposes a value with its ballot number. If the leader gets the majority to accept its proposal then the value is accepted and sites decide on that value with the corresponding ballot number. In Figure 2.7, we illustrate the communication patterns in Paxos between the different processes.

2.1.7   CAP THEOREM

Brewer [2000] proposed the following theorem, which was later proven by Gilbert and Lynch [2002]: A distributed shared data system can have at most two of following three properties:

1. Consistency (C)

2. Availability (A)

3. Tolerance to network Partitions (P)

This theorem has became known as the *CAP theorem*. In general, the common wisdom in large cloud-based data centers requires that for large scale operations the distributed system should tolerate partitioning, and hence the CAP theorem implies that during a network partition, a choice has to be made between consistency and availability. Traditional database systems choose consistency, while often, more recent data repositories, such as key-value stores, prefer availability. Brewer [2012] evaluates the ramifications of the CAP theorem, and emphasizes several of the nuances of that two-out-of-three aspect of the theorem. In particular, given that partitioning failures are not common, it is possible to design the system that allows *both* consistency and availability most of the time, and when a partitioning failure occurs, a strategy would be used to detect the partitioning, and then develop the most appropriate strategy to deal with the situation. Another important aspect that is emphasized is the strong relationship between latency and partitioning, namely, that the partitioning is assumed due to timeout, and hence from a practical point of view partitioning failures are assumed in a time bounded manner. This aspect is further amplified by Gilbert and Lynch [2012], where the CAP theorem is used as an illustration of the general trade-off between *safety* and *liveness* in an unreliable distributed system, and thus its close relationship to the impossibility of distributed consensus in an asynchronous system in the presence of failures [Fischer et al., 1983].

2.2   PEER TO PEER SYSTEMS

As an alternative to the traditional client-server model, the peer-to-peer (P2P) architecture presents a viable approach, and many of the techniques developed in P2P systems have been used quite successfully in data centers. The main goal in P2P systems is to make billions of objects available to millions of concurrent users, e.g., music files. To achieve this, a virtual or logical *overlay* is imposed on the physical network. Abstractly, an overlay organizes the way different sites communicate with each other as well as the storing of data objects at the different sites. In its simplest form, an object is viewed as a *key-value* pair. Overlays provide a method for retrieving objects, and typically support two basic operations: Given a key and a value, *insert* the key-value tuple in the overlay, and given a key, *lookup* and return the corresponding value. Overlays are typically represented as a graph, with sites as nodes, and edges connecting these sites, and can be categorized into *unstructured* and *structured* overlays.

Unstructured overlays impose no specific structure on the logical graph between the peers. The simplest such P2P design is the centralized approach, first used by Napster [Carlsson and Gustavsson, 2001], where a centralized server stores a database of all keys and the identities of the network nodes where these keys are located. This centralized server is consulted whenever searching for a key-value tuple. Napster was launched in 1999, peaked at 1.5 million simultaneous users, and then was shut down in July 2001 due to legal reasons.

Alternatively, a distributed design was used by Gnutella (http://en.wikipedia.org/wiki/Gnutella), where each node has several neighbors, and stores several keys in its local database. When asked to find a key k, a site checks in its local database if k is locally available. If yes, then return the corresponding value, if not, the site asks its neighbors recursively. Typically, a limiting threshold is used to limit unbounded propagation of the messages.

Structured overlays, on the other hand, impose a well-defined data structure on the various peers. Such a data structure is often referred to as a *Distributed Hash Tables (DHTs)*, which maps objects to sites, and provides methods for efficiently retrieving an object, given its corresponding key. In particular, in a structured overlay, edges are chosen according to some rule, and data is stored at pre-defined sites. Typically, each site also maintains a table that defines the next-hop for lookup operations. We will illustrate structured overlays with one of the most popular P2P systems called *Chord* [Stoica et al., 2001]. In Chord, each node is hashed using a *consistent hash function*, e.g., SHA-

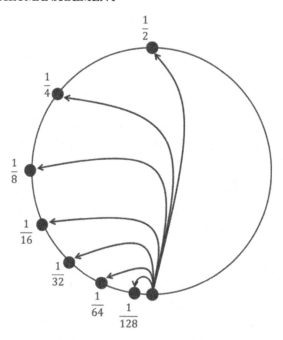

Figure 2.8: Finger table pointers in Chord.

1, to an m-bit identifier space (2^m IDs), where m is typically 160. Sites are then organized in a logical ring according to their IDs. Keys are also hashed into the same identifier space, and the key (and the corresponding value) is stored at its successor, i.e., the node with next higher ID.

Consistent hashing guarantees that for any set of n nodes and k keys, a node is responsible for at most $(1 + \epsilon)k/n$ keys. Furthermore, when a node joins or leaves, the responsibility for $O(k/n)$ keys are moved. To support efficient and scalable lookups, each node in the system maintains a *finger table*. The ith entry in the finger table of node n is the first node that succeeds or equals $n + 2^i$. Figure 2.8 illustrates the pointers of a given node in its finger table, with respect to the size of the network. In other words, the ith finger points $1/2^{(n-i)}$ way around the ring. Upon receiving a query for item id, a node checks whether it stores the item locally. If not, it forwards the query to the largest node in its finger table that does not exceed id. Assuming uniform node distribution around the Chord ring, the number of nodes in the search space is halved at each step. Hence, the expected number of hops is $O(\log n)$ where n is the number of nodes in the Chord ring.

2.3   DATABASE SYSTEMS

In this section we provide a fairly abstract, succinct, and high-level description of some basic background on some of the main concepts developed in database systems. Our formalism follows Bernstein et al. [1987]. A database knowledgeable reader can skip this section.

2.3.1 PRELIMINARIES

A database consists of a set of objects referred to as x, y, z. We assume each object has a value and the values of all the objects form the state of the database. Typically, these states must satisfy the database integrity constraints. Database objects support two atomic operations: *read* of x and *write* of x, or $r[x]$ and $w[x]$. The notion of a *transaction* is critical in database systems. A transaction is a set of operations executed in some partial order. The operations executed by transaction t_i are referred to as $r_i[x]$ and $w_i[x]$. A transaction is assumed to be correct, i.e., if executed alone on a consistent database, it transforms it into another consistent state.

Transaction execution must be *atomic*, i.e., it must ensure the following two properties:

1. No interference among transactions.

2. Either all its operations are executed or none.

A transaction t_i ends with a *commit* (c_i) or an *abort* (a_i) operation. A *concurrency control* protocol ensures that concurrent transactions do not interfere with each other. A *recovery protocol* ensures the all-or-nothing property.

Two operations are said to *conflict* if the order of execution is important, i.e., if one of them is a *write*. Given a set of transactions T, a *history H* over T is a partial order over all transaction operations and the order reflects the operation execution order (transaction order and conflicting operations order).

A database management system must ensure the so-called *ACID* properties, i.e.,

ATOMICITY. All-or-none property of each transaction

CONSISTENCY. Each transaction is a consistent unit of execution

ISOLATION. Transactions are isolated from the side-effects of other transactions

DURABILITY. Effects of transactions are persistent forever

The notion of correctness when a set of concurrent transactions is executed is premised on the fact that each transaction is consistent (C in $ACID$), and therefore, if executed in isolation, will take the database from a consistent state to another consistent state. Hence, give a set of transactions, we are guaranteed correctness if they are executed *serially*. In particular, a history H is *serial* if for any two transactions t_i and t_j in H, all operations of t_i are ordered in H before all operations of t_j or vice-versa.

To allow some degree of concurrency among transactions, the notion of *serializability* was developed. A history is serializable if it is equivalent to a serial history over the same set of transactions.

Two histories are *view equivalent* if they have the same effects, i.e., same values are written by all transactions. Since we do not know what transactions write, transactions are required to read from the same transactions and final written values are the same. Unfortunately, recognizing view serializable

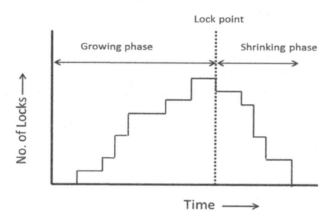

Figure 2.9: The two phases of Two-phase locking.

histories is NP-Complete [Papadimitriou, 1979]. Hence, a stronger notion of serializability was developed, namely, *conflict serializability*.

Recall that two operations on the same object *conflict* if at least one of them is write operation. Two histories H_1 and H_2 are *conflict equivalent* if they are defined over the same set of operations (and therefore same set of transactions) and they order the conflicting operations in the same order in both histories. A history H is *conflict serializable* if it is conflict equivalent to some serial history H_S. Since serial execution is correct, this ensures that a conflict serializable history is correct.

2.3.2   CONCURRENCY CONTROL

A concurrency control protocol must ensure conflict serializability. Concurrency control protocols are, in general, divided into *pessimistic* protocols, which use locking to avoid incorrect executions, and *optimistic* protocols, which use *certifiers* or *validator* at commit time to ensure correctness. In general, from a technical point of view, any concurrency control protocol can be easily extended for the distributed setting.

Locking Protocols

For each operation the transaction (or a concurrency control scheduler on its behalf) requests a lock. Each lock is requested in a specific mode: *read* or *write*. Two read locks are compatible, however, two write locks, as well as a read and a write lock are not compatible. If the data item is not locked in an incompatible mode the lock is granted. Otherwise, there is a lock conflict and the transaction becomes blocked (suffers a lock wait) until the current lock holder releases the lock. After an operation is executed, the lock is released. Locking by itself is not enough to ensure correctness. The *two phase locking* protocol add the following condition, which is sufficient to ensure conflict serializability [Eswaran et al., 1976]:

- Once a transaction has released a lock, it may not subsequently obtain any more locks on any data item.

Figure 2.9 provides an illustration of the increasing number of locks a transaction acquires during its growing phase, and the decreasing number of locks during the decreasing phase.

Two phase locking is very popular commercially, especially its *strict* version, which keeps all locks until the end of the transaction, i.e., until it commits or aborts. Two phase lock however does suffer from deadlocks. Also, data contention can arise due to queues on the data items, which form due to conflicting operations. Such contention may cause locking to result in thrashing (in regular multiprogramming systems, resource contention arises over memory, processors, I/O channels, etc., but not on data).

Optimistic Protocols

As mentioned above, locking may block resources for long periods. Optimistic concurrency control tries to avoid such blocking by allowing transactions to execute all their operations, and then uses a certification method to check if any conflicting operations had been executed by other transactions. In its simplest case, a transaction t_1 executes all its operations (write operations result in local cache updates). At commit, the scheduler checks if any active transaction has executed a conflicting operation, if so, abort t_1.

Kung and Robinson [1981] expanded on this simple idea by executing each transaction t_1 in three phases:

Read phase. During this phase transactions are allowed unrestricted reading of any object, writes are all local.

Validation phase. During this phase the scheduler ensures that no conflicts occurred by checking all concurrent transactions t_2, i.e., by checking whether the set of objects written by t_2 during its write phase overlap with the set of objects read by t_1 during its read phase. If so, t_1 is aborted.

Write phase. After successful validation, write values are written into the database.

A simple correctness argument can be used to demonstrate that optimistic concurrency control ensure serializable execution of transactions. Numerous variants of this protocol have been proposed, and optimistic protocol is being increasingly used in the cloud computing environments since it does not result in exclusive locks on data resources.

2.3.3   RECOVERY AND COMMITMENT

Centralized Recovery

Recovery from failures is an integral part of database management systems. The problem of centralized recovery, i.e., ensuring persistence or durability in the case of a single site database is handled by storing all data on disk. To recover from failures while ensuring atomicity, various mechanisms have been developed, all of which use the persistent storage device, i.e., the disk, during transaction execution to ensure the all-or-nothing property. The three main approaches are:

1. **Shadow paging**: where two copies of the database are kept on disk, one to be updated by the transaction, and when it commits, an atomic pointer switches to the new database copy.

2. **Before images**: where a disk log is used to store the *before-images* of all updated data items, and the transaction update the physical database immediately. If failure occurs and the transaction has not committed, then the database is restored to its original state based on log.

3. **After images**: where all updates are performed in a log of *after images*. If the transaction commits, then all the after images are installed in the database from the log.

Various recovery methods have been proposed based on these basic concepts. These methods combine before and after image logging in different ways for better performance for either committed or aborted transactions [Bernstein and Newcomer, 2009, Gray and Reuter, 1992, Weikum and Vossen, 2001].

The main challenge when moving from a centralized database to a distributed database, i.e., one where the objects may reside on different sites, is to ensure atomicity across different sites in the presence of failure. We now provide highlights of the main distributed commitment protocols.

Atomic Commitment

The fundamental problem of commitment arises due to the fact that transactions operate on multiple servers. Global commit needs unanimous local commits of all participants. Distributed systems may fail partially, in particular, the server may crash, and in the more extreme case, the network may fail, causing network partitioning. This may potentially result in inconsistent decisions, namely, a transaction commits at some servers but is aborted at some other servers.

The basic atomic commitment protocol is a simple distributed handshake protocol known as *two-phase commit (2PC)* [Gray, 1978]. In this protocol, a *coordinator* (the transaction manager) takes the responsibility of the unanimous decision: COMMIT or ABORT. All other database servers, which are executing the transaction are the *participants* in this protocol and become dependent on the coordinator. At commit time, the coordinator requests votes from all participants. Atomic commitment requires that all processes reach the same decision, in particular the transaction is committed only if all processes vote *yes*. Hence, if there are no failures and all processes vote *yes*, the decision will be to commit.

The protocol is executed as follows. The coordinator sends a *vote-request* to all participants. When a participant receives a *vote-request* message, it responds with either a *yes* or a *no* message, depending on whether it can locally commit or needs to abort the transaction (due to deadlock or failure to write on disk its local operations). The coordinator collects all votes. If all votes are *yes* then the transaction is considered committed, else it is aborted. The coordinator then sends the decision to all participants, who accordingly commit or abort the transaction locally.

What does a site do if it does not receive a message it is expecting? Note that this protocol assumes that the distributed system is synchronous, and hence there is a *timeout* mechanism. There are three cases to consider.

1. *Participant waiting for a vote-request.* In this case, it is safe for the participant to locally abort the transaction.

2. *Coordinator waiting for a vote.* In this case, the coordinator can also safely abort the transaction.

3. *Participant waiting for a decision.* This is a problematic case, and the participant is said to be *uncertain* as the transaction may have been either committed or aborted, and this particular participant might not be aware of the actual decision. It is interesting to note that the coordinator is never uncertain.

We now explore the case of the uncertain participant in more detail. In fact, this participant might be able to find help from the other participants by sending them a request for the decision. If any participant has committed or aborted, then it sends it the commit or abort decision. If a participant has not yet voted then it is safe to abort the transaction and send abort decision to all other participants. However, if all participants voted *yes* then all live participants are uncertain. In this case, the transaction is considered *blocked*, and all live participants need to wait until enough sites recover for the decision on this transaction to be recovered. The basic intuition is that a live participant is in an uncertain state, some other (failed) participants may be in commit and others in abort states. In general, the two phase commit protocol may suffer from blocking even in the case of simple crash failures.

To overcome the problem of blocking, an intermediate buffer state can be introduced so that if any operational site is uncertain, no process can have decided to commit [Skeen and Stonebraker, 1983]. The resulting protocol, called *three phase commit* is nonblocking in the presence of site failures. However, three phase commit cannot tolerate partitioning failures. In fact, it can be proven that there is no non-blocking atomic commitment protocol in the presence of partitioning failures [Skeen and Stonebraker, 1983].

In conclusion, commit protocols in distributed databases cause both significant complexity, as well as the potential for blocking. In fact, the failures of other sites may cause local data to become unavailable. Overall, distributed databases require significant overhead in managing correct executions. This reliance on a global synchronization mechanism limits scalability and has a significant impact on fault-tolerance and data availability. A combination of all these factors as well as others (related to authority over data at different sites) has led to the lack of significant commercial adoption of distributed databases.

CHAPTER 3

Cloud Data Management: Early Trends

With the growing popularity of the Internet, many applications and services started being delivered over the Internet and the scale of these applications also increased rapidly. As a result, many Internet companies, such as Google, Yahoo!, and Amazon, faced the challenge of serving hundreds of thousands to millions of concurrent users with ever increasing demands for data. Classical RDBMS technologies could not scale to these workloads while using commodity hardware, hence they were no longer viable for hosting such applications. The need for low cost scalable DBMSs resulted in the advent of the key-value stores such as Google's Bigtable [Chang et al., 2006], Yahoo!'s PNUTS [Cooper et al., 2008], and Amazon's Dynamo [DeCandia et al., 2007].[1] These systems were designed to scale out to thousands of commodity servers, replicate data across geographically remote data centers, and ensure high availability of user data in the presence of failures, which is the norm in such large infrastructures of commodity hardware. These requirements were a higher priority for the designers of the Key-value stores than rich functionality. Key-value stores support a simple *key-value*-based data model and single atomic key-value access guarantees, which were enough for their initial target applications [Vogels, 2007].

In this chapter, we discuss the design of these three systems and analyze the implications of the various design choices made by these systems. We start the chapter with a brief high-level overview of Bigtable, PNUTS, and Dynamo to familiarize the reader with their basic design. Section 3.2 distills some of the common design principles among different Key-value stores and the ramifications of these principles on different implementation approaches. Section 3.3 presents a more detailed description of the three main Key-value stores, discussing how these systems use the different design alternatives and principles to implement the end-to-end system.

3.1 OVERVIEW OF KEY-VALUE STORES

Bigtable [Chang et al., 2006] was designed to support Google's crawl and indexing infrastructure. A Bigtable cluster consists of a set of servers that serve the data; each such server (called a *tablet server*) is responsible for parts of the tables (known as a *tablet*). A tablet is logically represented as a key range and physically represented as a set of *SSTables*. A tablet is the unit of distribution and load balancing. Each tablet server has unique read-write access to a given tablet. Data from

---

[1]At the time of writing, various other Key-value stores (such as HBase, Cassandra, Voldemort, MongoDB etc.) exist in the open-source domain. However, most of these systems are variants of the three in-house systems discussed in this book.

the tables are persistently stored in the Google File System (GFS) [Ghemawat et al., 2003] that provides the abstraction of a scalable, consistent, fault-tolerant storage. There is no replication of user data inside Bigtable; all replication is handled by the underlying GFS layer. Coordination and synchronization between the tablet servers and metadata management is handled by a *master* and a Chubby cluster [Burrows, 2006]. Chubby provides the abstraction of a synchronization service via exclusive timed leases. Chubby guarantees fault-tolerance through log-based replication, and consistency amongst the replicas is guaranteed through the Paxos protocol [Chandra et al., 2007]. The Paxos protocol [Lamport, 1998] guarantees safety in the presence of different types of failures and ensures that the replicas are all consistent even when some replicas fail. But the high consistency comes at a cost: the limited scalability of Chubby due to the high cost of the Paxos protocol. Bigtable, therefore, limits interactions with Chubby to only the metadata operations.

PNUTS [Cooper et al., 2008] was designed by Yahoo! with the goal of providing efficient read access to geographically distributed clients. Data organization in PNUTS is also in terms of range-partitioned tables. PNUTS performs explicit replication across different data centers. This replication is handled by a guaranteed ordered delivery publish/subscribe systems called the Yahoo! Message Broker (**YMB**). PNUTS uses per record mastering and the master is responsible for processing the updates; the master is the publisher to YMB and the replicas are the subscribers. An update is first published to the YMB associated to the record's master. YMB ensures that updates to a record are delivered to the replicas in the order they were executed at the master, thus guaranteeing *single object timeline consistency*. PNUTS allows clients to specify the freshness requirements for reads. A read that does not have freshness constraints can be satisfied from any replica copy. Any read request that requires data that is more up-to-date than that of a local replica must be forwarded to the master.

Dynamo [DeCandia et al., 2007] was designed by Amazon to support the shopping carts for Amazon's e-commerce business. In addition to scalability, high write availability, even in the presence of network partitions, is a key requirement for Amazon's shopping cart application. In Dynamo data are organized using a distributed hash table, similar to Chord [Stoica et al., 2001] ring structure. Consistent hashing is used to distribute the data among the various servers on the ring. Dynamo explicitly replicates data, and a write request can be processed by any of the replicas. It uses a quorum of servers for serving the read and writes. A write request is acknowledged to the client when a quorum of replicas has acknowledged the write. To support high availability, the write quorum size can be set to one. Since updates are propagated asynchronously without any ordering guarantees, Dynamo only supports eventual replica consistency [Vogels, 2009] with the possibility that the replicas might diverge. Dynamo relies on application-level reconciliation based on vector clocks [Lamport, 1978].

3.2   DESIGN CHOICES AND THEIR IMPLICATIONS

Even though all three Key-value stores share some common goals, they differ significantly in some fundamental aspects of their designs. We now discuss these differences, the rationale for these decisions, and their implications. We focus on the design aspects. The performance implications of these difference are discussed elsewhere by Cooper et al. [2010].

3.2.1   DATA MODEL

The distinguishing feature of the Key-value stores is their simple data model. The primary abstraction is a table of items (or records) where each item is a *key-value* pair or a row. In this abstraction, each record is identified by a unique key, and the value can vary in its structure. The simplest, *Blob Data Model*, is one where the value is an uninterpreted binary string object, i.e., a blob. A more structured *Relational Data Model* approach for the value is a flat row-like structure similar to the relational model, where the value is structured into multiple columns, each with its own attribute (or key) name. Finally, the *Column Family Data Model* is one where the columns in the value field are grouped together into *column families*, each consisting of a set of columns. Multiple versions of each record in the key-value store can be maintained and indexed by a system or a user-defined timestamp. Furthermore, the table can be replicated in its entirety across multiple servers. Read and write (get and put) operations are typically supported in an atomic manner on each record in the key-value store. In some cases atomic read-modify-writes are also supported. In systems with a relational or a column family data store, some relational operations are supported such as selection and projection, but are restricted to a single table, and typically updates and deletes need to specify the primary key of the relevant key-value record. In general, no guarantees are provided for accesses spanning multiple key-value pairs.

In general, these systems allow large rows, thus allowing the logical entity to be represented as a single row. However, a single row typically can reside in a single server. Restricting data accesses to a *single* key provides designers the flexibility of operating at a much finer granularity. In the presence of such restrictions, application-level data manipulation is restricted to a single compute node boundary and thus obviates the need for multi-node coordination and synchronization [Helland, 2007]. As a result, these systems can scale to billions of key-value pairs using *horizontal partitioning* or *sharding*, where the rows of the key-value store are distributed among multiple servers. The rows stored at a server are often referred to as *shards* or em chunks. The rationale is that even though there can be potentially millions of requests, the requests are generally distributed throughout the data set. Moreover, the single key operation semantics limits the impact of failure to only the data that were being served by the failed node; the rest of the nodes in the system can continue to serve requests. Furthermore, single-key operation semantics allow fine-grained partitioning and load-balancing. This is different from RDBMSs that consider data as a cohesive whole and a failure in one component results in overall system unavailability.

3.2.2   DATA DISTRIBUTION AND REQUEST ROUTING

To ensure flexible scaling out to multiple servers, a key-value store needs to partition the data to distribute it over a cluster of servers. In general, a table is partitioned into *tablets* (similar to *shards or chunks*), which form the units of distribution and load balancing. The two main approaches for partitioning are *range partitioning* and *hash partitioning*. Range partitioning typically orders all records lexicographically based on the key, and then divides the objects on different servers in that order. Hash partitioning hashes the records based on the key to linear address space, which is then divided among the different servers. A typical hashing approach can use a distributed hash table (DHT) such as Chord [Stoica et al., 2001], as discussed in Chapter 2.

To retrieve a particular key-value record, the system must also have a routing mechanism to determine which server is serving the particular record. In general, the approach can be divided into centralized and distributed solutions. In a centralized approach, specialized mechanisms are needed to route the client requests, for example, the routing logic can be stored in a client library that is provided to each client, or is stored in a specialized set of routing servers to which requests are routed. Irrespective of the partitioning method, the domain can be divided into intervals (the original domain in the case of range partitioning and the hash domain in the case of hash partition). The routing logic can then either contain the entire mapping of key intervals to the servers, or can have a pointer to an index structure, typically a hierarchical or B-Tree-like structure. In the decentralized approach, the client requests are routed using consistent hashing among a distributed peer-to-peer organization of the servers.

3.2.3   CLUSTER MANAGEMENT

Key-value stores are designed to store large data sets on clusters of servers in large data centers. As the scale of the system increases, managing such clusters without human intervention becomes a challenge. Specifically, detecting and recovering from failures, and basic load balancing functionalities are critical to the system's proper operation. Different key-value stores use different approaches for managing clusters of servers, however, in general, there are two main design approaches: a centralized master-based approach, and a decentralized distributed approach.

In the *master-based approach*, a designated server is chosen as a master. This master keeps track of all data servers using a highly available fault-tolerant service. This service helps manage the data servers and keeps track of the data stored at the different servers. A data server obtains *leases* with this service for the data it manages. When a data server fails, its leases are lost, and the service reports this failure. On the detection of a failure, the master can reassign the data to new servers. Finally, if the master fails, a new master is elected to take over.

In the decentralized approach, gossip messages are typically used to enable each server to learn about the failure or recovery of a server. Gossip messages are typically messages that are communicated among servers on a continuous basis, and contain relevant performance measurements. The failure of a server is detected when a gossip message from that server is missing. The centralized approach is more vulnerable to unavailability in the presence of failures of some critical components, while the decentralized approach allows the system to be less susceptible to specific failures, but at the cost of a more complex design as well as increase in message overhead.

3.2.4   FAULT-TOLERANCE AND DATA REPLICATION

Key-value stores are typically stored in large data centers containing thousands of commodity servers. Such servers are prone to failures. Key-value stores were therefore designed to handle failures gracefully to ensure high data availability. In general, fault-tolerance is handled by replicating data on multiple servers. To ensure fault-tolerance in the presence of catastrophic, large-scale failures, such as earthquakes, tsunamis, etc, geographic replication is used, i.e., copies of the data are stored at different data centers, which are geographically separated. In general, replication is either implicit or explicit.

In the *implicit replication approach*, data management is separated from the storage component. The data management component is in charge of accessing the data or records, i.e., controls read and write accesses. The actual reading and writing of the data is managed by an independent entity, typically a distributed file system. The distributed file system manages the data blocks, which are replicated and managed by the file system, while providing APIs to the data management component to allow the reading and writing of the data.

In the *explicit replication approach* the management of the various copies of a data item is managed explicitly by the data management component, i.e., by the component that executes the read and write operations. Depending on where the copies are located and the degree of consistency that is supported by the system, different mechanisms have been proposed. Typically, for each object, a copy is designated as the master, and is used for reading and writing. For write operations, once the master is updated, the rest of the copies are updated asynchronously. Alternatively, read and write quorums can be defined on the copies. If both read and write quorums intersect, as well as if any two write quorums intersect, then the data is always consistent, and readers access the most up-to-date copies. However, for efficiency, quorums might not intersect, in which case inconsistencies may arise. Detecting and fixing such inconsistent data copies is an interesting topic, and various proposals have been made. Typically, they use a version vector, with an entry corresponding to the number of updates for a given copy. If there is a divergence in the version vectors, they are considered inconsistent, and the application needs to be consulted to reconcile the different copies.

When replication is supported, various models have been proposed:

- *Strong Consistency*, where all copies of a given record have identical values as far as read or get operations are concerned.

- *Weak Consistency*, where different copies might have different and conflicting values. In this case, reconciliation methods need to be developed to allow the application or the system to determine the correct value of the record. One simple mechanism for detecting inconsistencies is *vector clocks*, where each copy has a vector associated with it, and each entry in the vector reflects the number of updates corresponding to that copy. If the vector of one copy is greater than or equal to another vector, then the copies are consistent, otherwise, there is a conflict and reconciliation is needed.

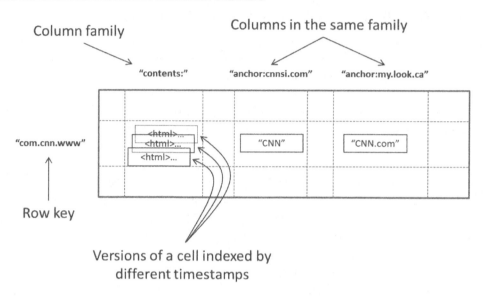

Figure 3.1: Bigtable data model.

- *Timeline Consistency*, which ensures that all copies of a record apply all updates in the same order. Using this consistency model, read operations can be specified to return any version of the record, the most up-to-date version, or even a specific version.

- *Eventual Consistency*, where updates are eventually propagated to all the copies, and eventually, all copies have the same values, but in the meantime, older or stale versions might be accessible for reading.

Typically, scalability and high availability are the foremost requirements for Key-value stores. As we discussed before, the CAP theorem states that a distributed system can only choose two of consistency, availability, and partition tolerance. For systems spanning large infrastructures or geographically separated data centers, network partitions are inevitable. In the event of a network partition, these systems usually choose availability over replica consistency.

3.3   KEY-VALUE STORE SYSTEM EXAMPLES

We now discuss in more detail three different key-value stores, namely, Bigtable, PNUTS, and Dynamo, and highlight how the different design principles discussed in the previous section were implemented.

3.3.1   BIGTABLE

Bigtable [Chang et al., 2006] was developed by Google as a data store for many of its applications including web indexing, Google Earth, and Google Finance. Bigtable is arguably the first large-scale key-value store used in a commercial setting. Its data model is a Column Family Data Model which is quite general, and can be viewed as a sparse multi-dimensional sorted map where a single data item is identified by a row identifier, a column family, a column, and a timestamp. The row keys are arbitrary strings, which can be up to 64K bytes, although most keys are typically in the 10 to 100 bytes size range. A column family is a set of column keys, and they form the unit of data co-location and access at the storage layer. All data stored in a column family are usually of the same type. Furthermore, a column family must be created before any data are inserted in the column value. Each cell in Bigtable can contain multiple versions of the same data and these versions are indexed by timestamp, which can be assigned by Bigtable, or explicitly by the client. Figure 3.1 shows an example of Bigtable that shows a row corresponding to an entry referring to the web page of cnn.com. This example has two column families: one for *contents* and another for anchors. The cnn row has two anchor columns: one for Sports Illustrated and another for My-look home pages. Also note that the contents column has three timestamped versions.

Bigtable provides APIs for creating and deleting tables and column families, as well as their metadata, e.g., access control rights. It also provides clients with primitives to lookup, write, and delete values, as well as iterate over a subset of the records. Every read and write operation of a value defined by a single key is atomic, irrespective of the number of columns being read. In addition, single row transactions that atomically read-modify-write a single row are supported, but not multi-row transactions.

Bigtable orders the data lexicographically based on the row key, and divides the data into *tablets*, which are the unit of distribution and load balancing. These tablets are assigned to *tablet servers*, which handle all read and write requests to its tablets. A special *master server* assigns tablets to these tablet servers and is responsible for tablet server load balancing, as well as for detecting the addition and deletion of tablet servers. The *tablet servers* are responsible for managing accesses to the tablets, which are physically stored as *SSTables* in Google's distributed file systems, *Google File System (GFS)*. GFS provides Bigtable with a strongly consistent replicated storage abstraction. The GFS design, however, is optimized for replication within a data center. As a result, a large-scale data center level outage results in data unavailability in Bigtable.

Bigtable uses a highly available, fault-tolerant lock service called *Chubby* for managing the tablet servers. Chubby provides a namespace that consists of directories and small files. Each directory or file can be used as a lock, and reads and writes to a file are atomic. A Chubby service consists of five active replicas, which are kept consistent using Paxos. The service is live when a majority of the replicas are running and can communicate with each other.

The master server uses the Chubby service to perform cluster management. The master and every tablet server in the system obtains a timed lease with Chubby that must be periodically renewed. A server in a Bigtable cluster can carry out its responsibilities only if it has an active lease

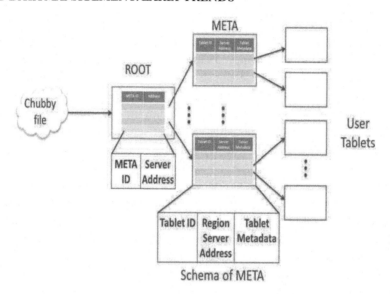

Figure 3.2: Request routing in Bigtable (adapted from [Chang et al., 2006]).

from Chubby. Every tablet server periodically reports to the master using heartbeat messages that also contain the load statistics. These heartbeat messages and the leases with Chubby form the basis for failure detection and recovery. After a tablet server failure is detected by the master, the state of the failed server can be recovered from GFS at another live tablet servers.

Bigtable uses the hierarchical approach to locate data: it uses a three-level $B+$-tree structure (called the ROOT tablet, the META tablets, and the USER tables) that stores the interval mapping, and which is illustrated in 3.2. The first level is a file stored in Chubby that contains the location of the root tablet. The root tablet has the locations of the metadata tablets, which points to the locations of the user tablets. Each Bigtable client maintains a client library that caches tablet locations. If the data is stale, the client uses the hierarchical structure to retrieve the tablet locations.

Client updates are committed to a write ahead log that stores redo records and is stored in GFS. Recently committed updates are stored in an in-memory buffer called a memtable. A write operation is executed by first checking if the client has privileges for the write operation (from Chubby). A log record is then generated to the commit log file of redo records. Once the write commits, its contents are inserted into the memtable. A read operation also first checks that the client has the correct privileges, then the read is performed on a merged view of the SSTables that constitute the tablet, and the recent updates in memtable.

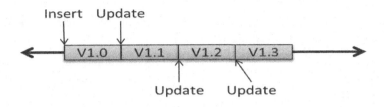

Figure 3.3: Per-record timeline used to provide timeline consistency for updates.

3.3.2   PNUTS

PNUTS [Cooper et al., 2008] was built to provide database support for Yahoo!'s web applications. PNUTS provides a traditional flat row-like database structure similar to the relational model. Schemas are flexible and allow new attributes to be added at any time, and records do not need to have values for all attributes. PNUTS exposes to the users a simple relational model with single table scans restricted with predicates. Hence, compared to the relational query model, PNUTS only supports selections and projections on a single table, and does not enforce any referential integrity constraints. Also, updates and deletes must specify the primary key. As with similar early key-value stores, atomicity and isolation are supported at the granularity of a single key-value pair, i.e. atomic read/write and atomic read-modify-write are possible to only individual key-value pairs. No guarantees are provided for accesses spanning multiple data key-value pairs. PNUTS provides *per-record timeline consistency*, which ensures that when a record is replicated on multiple sites (often geographically dispersed), all copies of a record apply all updates in the same order. Using this consistency model, read operations can be specified to return any version of the record, the most up to date version, or even a specific version. For example, in Figure 3.3, a record is created, as version V1.0, and is then updated multiple times resulting in the creation of versions V1.1, V1.2 and V1.3. A read operation that requires the latest version would read version V1.3, otherwise, a specific version can be specified. Furthermore, PNUTS provides an atomic test-and-set operation which ensures that the write operation is executed only if a desired version on the object is the current version.

A PNUTS system is divided into regions, where each region has a full copy of all the data (Figure 3.4). Typically, regions are geographically distributed to ensure fault-tolerance in the face of catastrophic failures at a single data center. Data tables are horizontally partitioned based on their primary key into *tablets*, which are stored in *storage units*. Data can be either hashed to the different tablets, or ranged partitioned. A special *router* keeps track of which tablet stores a given record by storing a mapping from intervals to servers. The interval mappings easily fit into memory, making them very efficient to search. Routers contain only a cached copy of the interval mapping. The mapping is owned by the *tablet controller*, and routers periodically poll the tablet controller to get any changes to the mapping. The tablet controller is responsible for detecting failures as well as deciding when to move tablets between storage units for load balancing or recovery, and when a large tablet must be split.

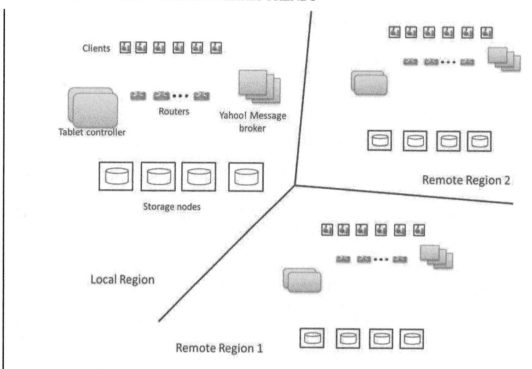

Figure 3.4: PNUTS architecture.

PNUTS uses the Yahoo! Message Broker (YMB) to update the different copies. An update is acknowledged to the client only after it has been replicated within YMB. PNUTS uses YMB as a fault-tolerant replicated log and leverages YMB's guaranteed ordered delivery for replication; and guarantees single record timeline consistency for the replicas. YMB ensures that all messages published by a given client are delivered to all regions in the same order, however, messages published concurrently by different clients may be delivered in different orders at different regions. To ensure timeline consistency, PNUTS uses a *per-record mastering* approach, where each record has a master, and different records in a table may have masters in different regions. All updates are directed to the master record, and then YMB is used to asynchronously propagate to the other copies. This approach was chosen to ensure low latency, as the master copy is chosen to be in the region with most update operations, and most web applications seem to exhibit significant write locality. If a record's master fails, another replica can be elected as the master once all updates from the original master's YMB have been applied to the replica, a mechanism called *re-mastering*. However, in the event of a data center outage resulting in YMB unavailability, similar to any asynchronous log-based replication protocol, the tail of the log that has not propagated to other data centers will be lost

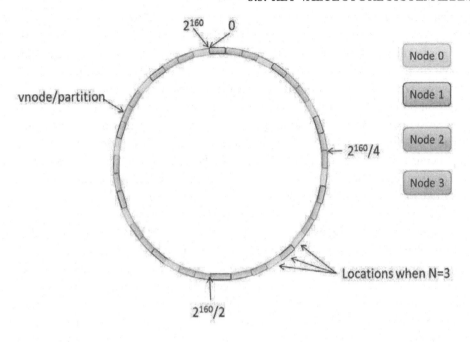

Figure 3.5: The P2P core of Dynamo with four virtual nodes.

if the records are re-mastered. Therefore, PNUTS presents a trade-off between data loss and data unavailability in the event of a catastrophic failure.

3.3.3 DYNAMO

Amazon runs large-scale e-commerce applications, and needs highly available storage. Dynamo [DeCandia et al., 2007] is one of its first key-value store systems. Compared to other proposals, Dynamo provides the simplest data model where each record is identified by a unique key, and the value is a binary object, i.e., a blob. Dynamo provides a *put* and a *get* operation, and provides no support for operations that span multiple objects. Dynamo uses a distributed peer-to-peer (**P2P**) approach for partitioning the data across different data storage servers. Its approach uses consistent hashing [Karger et al., 1997], where the output range of the hash function is a circular ring space, as in Chord [Stoica et al., 2001]. To ensure load balancing, instead of assigning each node to a single location in the ring, Dynamo introduces a notion of *virtual nodes*, where each physical node is mapped to multiple locations in the ring, thus providing better load distribution on the various physical servers (see Figure 3.5). By using consistent hashing to route the client requests, Dynamo obviates the need for explicit routing mechanisms.

To ensure high availability and durability, Dynamo replicates each data item on N storage nodes, namely, the node where the item is hashed to, and the $N-1$ clockwise successive nodes on the ring. The node handling a put or a get request is referred to as the *coordinator*, which is the node designated by the consistent hashing—typically the first of the n copies, but in the presence of failures, this might not be the case. Dynamo provides *eventual consistency*, where a put operation is executed on the coordinator node, and then asynchronously updates are propagated to the rest of the copies. Dynamo associates read and write quorums with get and put operations. When a put operation propagates its updates to the N copies, it waits for W nodes to acknowledge before considering the put operation successful. Likewise, a get operation sends its read request to all N copies and waits for R copies to respond before deciding which version to return as the value of the item being read. If $R + W$ is greater than N, then strong consistency is ensured. However, for high performance, Dynamo often does not require the intersection of read and write quorums (also referred to as *sloppy quorums*). As a result of sloppy quorums, multiple concurrent updates might be executed on the same object, giving rise to divergent versions of the same data item. To detect such inconsistencies, Dynamo uses vector clocks, and the application is passed these vector clocks to resolve any inconsistencies. Vector clocks capture causal dependencies between versions by associating a vector with each copy, consisting of a list of pairs, one for each replica, and the associated version number. Inconsistencies can be detected by comparing the vectors associated with any two versions or copies. For more permanent failures, and to detect and remedy more persistent failures, Dynamo uses *Merkel trees*. Merkel trees are hash trees where leaves hash to individual keys, and parents hash to their children allowing for fast and efficient detection of divergence between different replicas.

To handle the failure or addition of a node, Dynamo allows an administrator to explicitly issue a command to a Dynamo server to join or be removed from the system. When a new server joins the system it is assigned a random set of key-value items. Dynamo then depends on decentralized failure detection protocols that use simple gossip-based mechanisms that enable each server to learn about the arrival and departure of other servers. The gossip-based protocol requires each node to randomly pick another node with which to reconcile its membership changes histories. This ensure eventual consistency of view membership at the various nodes in the system.

3.4   DISCUSSION

In this chapter, we covered three key-value stores which represent three different approaches to designing such scalable data stores needed to serve applications storing and serving ever-growing amounts of data. All these systems were designed as *in-house* solutions by some large Internet companies. From the time these respective architectures were publicized, a number of open source projects have gained in maturity and popularity. The architecture of many of these open source projects were inspired by Bigtable and Dynamo. Examples of these systems include: HBase, Cassandra, Voldemort, Riak, CouchDB, MongoDB, and many more. Such systems have been broadly classified as key-value stores, where the value can be an un-interpreted stream of bytes (such as Voldemort) or can have a flexible and extensible structure (such as HBase and Cassandra) or document stores, where the values represent complex data such as JSON or other document formats. While many of the architectural features resemble the *in-house* systems, these open source systems often optimize their architectures based on the requirements posed by the applications these systems aim to serve. Cattell [2011] presents a thorough survey of the design space of such scalable key-value and document stores, collectively called *NoSQL* stores. Cooper et al. [2010] presents a performance analysis of a subset of these key-value stores to highlight some of the architectural difference and their impact on the performance of these systems.

Main memory object stores, such as Memcached [Danga Interactive Inc., 2012], form another class of key-value stores whose primary goal is to cache data in memory to minimize the response time for data accesses. For instance, when the key-value stores are not optimized for accesses based on secondary attributes. However, if an application issues certain queries that access these secondary attributes, results of such queries can be materialized in a caching service such as Memcached. In principle, many of the techniques used to design general purpose key-value stores can be used to build such distributed main memory key-value stores. With the decreasing cost of main memory, it is also conceivable to have the entire database in memory to allow fast access to large volumes of data. The RAMClouds project [Ousterhout et al., 2009] aims to develop such a distributed main memory database. Some interesting challenges arise when designing systems optimized to be resident in main memory. Ongaro et al. [2011] discuss one such challenge: fast recovery from node failure in a main memory database without full data replication. As data center networks become faster and memory becomes cheaper, such main memory database systems are expected to become mainstream for storing and serving big data.

CHAPTER 4

Transactions on Co-located Data

Key-value stores, such as Bigtable, PNUTS, and Dynamo, were designed to support single-operation and single data item transactions. Such operational semantics were sufficient for the initial set of applications for which these systems were designed. As these early data management platforms for the cloud became mature, an expanded set of applications used these systems, which naturally resulted in demands for greater accessibility to multiple data items. Furthermore, the logic of many applications is often expressed as multiple operations accessing multiple data items. The absence of transactional abstractions spanning multiple data items and operations considerably increased the application software complexity as well as the overhead on the application developers [Hamilton, 2010, Obasanjo, 2009]. Transactional access to data has been an important abstraction ever since the early days of relational database management systems. The transaction abstraction considerably simplifies application logic and reasoning about data integrity and correctness. As a result, the need for transactional abstractions increased at the same time as the need for scalable data management systems increased. Many systems have therefore been proposed and built that provide richer transactional semantics.

It is well understood that flexible general-purpose transactions would prevent the systems from scaling out to large numbers of nodes or span geographically distributed data centers. Therefore, most of the first attempts at incorporating transactional access resulted in systems that make a choice between limiting the granularity of transactional access (i.e., limit the scope of the data items that are accessed by a single transaction) or relaxing some transactional guarantees (such as supporting isolation levels weaker than serializability).

We broadly divide these systems into two classes. One class limits the execution of *most* (and if possible all) transactions to a single node. Such systems allow efficient non-distributed transaction execution, but often at the cost of constraining the application schema or data access patterns. These systems rely on *co-locating* data items that are frequently accessed together within a transaction. Another class of systems allows transactions to span multiple nodes. These systems often expose a more flexible transactional interface to the applications, though at the cost of making transaction execution more expensive. In this chapter, we survey the approaches and mechanisms for the former class of systems; we will cover the latter class of systems in the next chapter.

In addition to efficient transaction execution, limiting transactions to a single node results in a number of other benefits. First, it allows the system to scale-out by adding more servers and

distributing the transactional load across the servers. Minimizing distributed synchronization is critical to ensuring linear scalability. Second, it limits the effect of a failure to only the transactions executing on the failed nodes and minimizes the impact on the remaining nodes, thus allowing graceful performance degradation in the event of failures. Finally, with transaction executions limited to a single node, many techniques developed for optimizing transaction execution performance can be potentially applied.

In this chapter, we first analyze how the different schema and data access patterns can be leveraged to co-locate data or ownership to execute transactions locally at a single node (§ 4.1); *Ownership* refers to a node's exclusive read and write access to data items. This partitioning and co-location of data or ownership is the critical first step toward efficient non-distributed transaction execution. We then focus our discussion on the different techniques for transaction execution (§ 4.2), physical data storage (§ 4.3), and data replication (§ 4.4). Finally, we discuss several of the systems that use these design principles for scale-out transaction processing (§ 4.5).

4.1   DATA OR OWNERSHIP CO-LOCATION

Co-locating data frequently accessed together within a transaction allows the system to execute the transactions efficiently without incurring distributed synchronization. One design option is to leverage specific schema patterns and design applications conforming to these patterns by limiting the data items a transaction can access. Partitioning the data by analyzing the applications' access patterns and physically co-locating a partition's data at a single node is another design option. Both the aforementioned design options *statically* define the granule of transactional access and co-locate the data that form this granule. An alternative design option is to allow the application to *dynamically* specify the granule of transactional access while the system re-organizes ownership based on the application-specified partitions to allow transactions to execute locally within a node. In this section, we discuss all these design options in greater detail.

4.1.1   LEVERAGING SCHEMA PATTERNS

A common schema pattern that is amenable to data co-location and partitioning is a hierarchy of objects or tables where transactions access the data items forming this hierarchy. In this section, we present three variants of such schema patterns and describe how transaction accesses can be limited to a single node.

Tree Schema

A common example of a hierarchical schema is the *tree schema* illustrated in Figure 4.1. This schema supports three types of tables: the *primary* table, *secondary* tables, and *global* tables. The primary table forms the root of the tree; a schema has one primary table whose primary key also acts as the partitioning key. However, there can be multiple secondary and global tables. Every secondary table in a database schema will have the primary table's key as a foreign key. Referring to Figure 4.1(a), the key k_p of the primary table appears as a foreign key in each of the secondary tables. In contrast

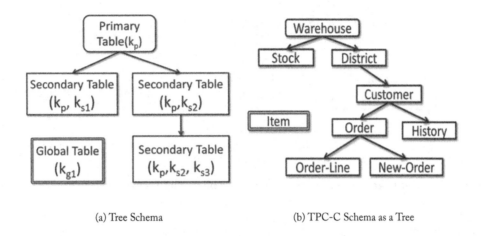

(a) Tree Schema   (b) TPC-C Schema as a Tree

Figure 4.1: The Tree schema is a representative hierarchical schema. The schema used in the TPC-C benchmark conforms to this tree structure.

to the two table types, global tables are look-up tables that are mostly read-only. Since global tables are updated infrequently, these tables can be replicated in all the partitions.

This tree structure implies that corresponding to every row in the primary table, there are a group of related rows in the secondary tables. We refer to these rows that reference the same key in the root table as a *row group*; all rows in the same row group can be co-located within a database partition. By limiting transactions to only access rows that have the same root table key, this design can ensure that transactions execute within a single node. Since global tables are replicated in all partitions, a transaction can also read any data item from a global table. The set of rows that reference the same database partition is a collection of such groups of related rows.

Figure 4.1(b) shows a representation of the TPC-C schema [TPC-C] as a tree schema. In the TPC-C schema, the WAREHOUSE table is the root of the schema with its primary key (w_id) being the partition key that is part of all other secondary tables. As can be seen in Figure 4.1(b), the TPC-C schema has seven secondary tables forming a tree of depth five. The ITEM table is the global table in the schema. According to the TPC-C benchmark specifications, a vast majority of the transactions (about 85%) access rows that are part of the same warehouse, and hence can be limited to a single partition. The TATP benchmark [Neuvonen et al., 2009] is another example conforming to the tree schema. The tree schema is amenable to partitioning using the partition key that is shared by all the tables in the schema. Such a pattern has been used for data partitioning in systems such as ElasTraS [Das et al., 2010a] and H-Store [Kallman et al., 2008].

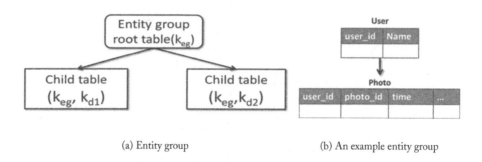

(a) Entity group   (b) An example entity group

Figure 4.2: Entity groups are another example of a hierarchical schema pattern.

Entity Groups

Another example of a hierarchical schema is an *entity group* (shown in Figure 4.2(a)) where each schema has a set of tables and each table is comprised of a set of entities. Each entity contains a set of properties which are named and typed values; a set of columns together form the primary key of the table. In the classical relational sense, entities are equivalent to rows in a table and properties are equivalent to strongly typed columns. Each table is either an *entity group root table* or a *child table*. Each child table has a foreign key relationship with the root table. Therefore, each child entity references exactly one entity in the root table, called the root entity. A root entity along with all child entities that reference it form an entity group. Evidently, all entities comprising an entity group can be physically co-located, thus allowing transactions accessing only a single entity group to execute non-distributed. This schema pattern is exploited in Megastore [Baker et al., 2011] to partition the database while ensuring that the data items frequently accessed together are co-located.

Figure 4.2(b) shows an example schema for a photo sharing application where USER is the root table and PHOTO is a child table; a user and its collection of all photos forms an entity group. Email accounts, blogs, and geographic data form natural examples of applications that can be modeled using the entity group abstraction.

Table Groups

While the tree schema and entity group impose a hierarchical structure, a generalization to this design pattern of schema-imposed data co-location is the notion of a *table group* which consists of a set of tables. A table group can have a partition key (equivalent to the key of the root table in the tree schema and entity group) in which case it is known as a *keyed* table group. However, a table group can also be *keyless*, which makes the table group structure more amorphous and generic compared to the tree schema and entity group. All tables in a keyed table group have a column named partition key which need not be unique in a given table. That is, a partition key need not be the primary key of any table. All rows in a table group that have the same partition key form a *row group*. In a keyed table group, a database partition can be formed as a set of row groups.

Address

Id	Add_Id	Street	...
1	101	427 Abc	
1	102	721 Main	
2	104	112 1ˢᵗ	

Customer

Id	Name	...
1	John	
2	Mary	

Order

Id	Oid	...
1	1001	
1	1002	
1	1003	
2	1010	

Figure 4.3: A *keyed* table group with a partition column (Id). All rows with the same partition key form a row group; different row groups are denoted with different background shades.

All data items part of a table group can be co-located. By requiring that transactions access only the data items within a single entity group, a system can eliminate distributed transactions. Such an abstraction forms the logical data model of Cloud SQL Server [Bernstein et al., 2011b] which is the data back-end for Microsoft's SQL Azure. In addition to restricting transactions to access a single table group, for a keyed table group, Cloud SQL Server requires that transactions access only a single row group. Figure 4.3 illustrates a keyed table group with three tables. As noted earlier, a keyed table group has a hierarchical structures, however, a table group is not required to have this hierarchical structure.

Discussion

The three schema patterns represent approaches that allow data co-location and limit access of most, if not all, transactions to data within a partition. Note that transactions spanning multiple partitions can still be supported, though at the cost of requiring distributed synchronization and thus higher execution cost. Except in a keyless table group, the remaining schema patterns define a small unit of data—-row group and entity group—-that constitutes the granule of consistent transactional access. There is tight coupling of data items within these granules, while different granules couple only loosely. A database partition combines a set of these granules, except in a keyless table group where the table group itself forms a partition.

In designs based on the keyed data granules, the key is also part of the granule's identity. The database can be partitioned by partitioning these keys by hashing, range partitioning, or using a lookup table to determine the partition a key belongs to. Furthermore, the loose coupling between the individual granules allows the system to dynamically split partitions or merge partitions corresponding to contiguous ranges. If rows are physically stored in the order by their partitioning key, such a split or merge is efficient and requires minimal data movement. For instance, in a range-partitioned

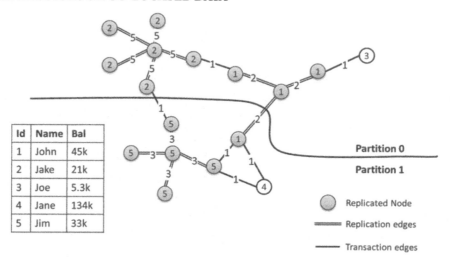

Id	Name	Bal
1	John	45k
2	Jake	21k
3	Joe	5.3k
4	Jane	134k
5	Jim	33k

Figure 4.4: Partitioning the database leveraging the application's access patterns by modeling the data and accesses using a weighted undirected graph.

database, if a range is split, the key that determines the logical split point directly corresponds to the boundary at which the partition is also physically split.

4.1.2   ACCESS-DRIVEN DATABASE PARTITIONING

While many applications can conform to a specified schema and access pattern, others are not amenable to such partitioning. An alternative design is to analyze the applications' access patterns to identify the data items which, when co-located within a partition, will limit most transactions to access only a single partition. The key idea is to partition an application's data by analyzing its workload. Curino et al. [2010] propose one such approach that models the application's data accesses as a graph and then uses well-known graph partitioning techniques to partition the graph, and hence the database.

The applications database and the workload is represented as a weighted undirected graph. We explain the steps for forming the graph using a simple application illustrated in Figure 4.4. Each tuple is represented as a node in the graph, edges connect tuples that are accessed within the same transaction, and edge weights account for the number of transactions that co-access a pair of tuples. For example, in Figure 4.4, tuples with id 1 and 3 are co-accessed by a single transaction and hence the edge between them has a weight of 1. Replication is represented by replacing a node by $n + 1$ nodes, where n is the number of transactions that *update* the tuple. For example, considering Figure 4.4, tuple id 2 is accessed by five transactions and is therefore represented by six nodes. The weights of the replication edges connecting each replica to the central node represent the cost of replicating the tuple. This cost is the number of transactions that *update* the tuple in the workload. The rationale for using updates as the weights for the replication edges is that when replicating a tuple, each read can be performed locally, but each update becomes a distributed transaction. This graph structure allows the partitioning algorithm to naturally balance the costs and the benefits of replication by minimizing the weight of edges that cross the partition boundaries. The graph partitioning strategy heuristically minimizes the cost of a graph cut, while balancing the weight of each partition. The weight of a partition is computed as the sum of the weights of the nodes assigned to that partition.

Once the database and the interactions are modeled as a graph, well-known graph partitioning algorithms can be used to cut this graph into k non-overlapping partitions such that the overall cost of the cut edges (i.e., the edges that cross the different cuts) is minimized. Essentially, this formulates partitioning as a variant of the minimum k-cut problem [Goldschmidt and Hochbaum, 1988]. The graph cut algorithm also keeps the weight of partitions within a constant factor of perfect balance where the degree of imbalance is a parameter. Since the weight of edges represent the number of accesses, this graph partition operation approximates minimizing the number of distributed transactions while balancing data size evenly across the partitions.

Contrary to range or hash-based partitioning, where the ranges or the hash function can be used to route the incoming requests to the correct partition that stores the data item, graph-based partitioning requires an additional step to establish the routing mechanism. One approach is to store a lookup table which is output by the partitioner. While a lookup table allows fine-grained partitioning, the overhead for storing, looking up, and maintaining this lookup table often becomes expensive, especially for very large databases. An alternative is to learn the mappings between a row to partitions as a compact model, such as decision trees. Partition discovery for a data item can be posed as a classification problem where the data item is the input and the partition label is the output. The training phase of the classifier determines the rules for partition discovery and represents it as a compact model. Given an unlabeled value, a label can be found by descending the tree, applying predicates at each node until a labeled leaf is reached. While the lookup table-based approach allows fine-grained partitioning, the decision tree-based approach results in coarse-grained partitioning which might result in a greater fraction of distributed transactions. A final validation phase determines the best strategy for a given workload. Curino et al. [2010] present various optimizations for scaling, such as sampling tuples and transactions, coalescing tuples that are always accessed together, and rejecting large scans that access a large fraction of the database.

4.1.3 APPLICATION-SPECIFIED DYNAMIC PARTITIONING

Many applications have static access patterns and hence are amenable to static partitioning of their databases. In the previous sections, we discussed approaches to statically partition the database, that is, the data items to be co-located within a partition are known upfront. Many applications, however, have fast evolving access patterns, thus negating the benefits of static partitioning based on access patterns. Consider the example of an online multi-player game, such as an online casino. An instance of the game has multiple players and the gaming application requires transactional access to the player profiles while the game is in progress. For example, every player profile might have an associated balance (in a real or virtual currency) and the balance of all players must be transactionally updated as the game proceeds.

To ensure the efficient execution of these transactions, it is imperative that the data items corresponding to the profiles are co-located within a database partition. However, a game instance lasts for small periods of time as players move from one game to another. Furthermore, over a period of time, a player might participate in game instances involving different groups of players. Therefore, the group of data items on which the application requires transactional access changes rapidly over time. In a statically partitioned system, the profiles of the players participating in a game instance might belong to different partitions. Providing transaction guarantees across these groups of player profiles will result in distributed transactions.

Efficient transactional access on such dynamically defined partitions requires an abstraction for lightweight ownership (or data) re-organization that minimizes distributed synchronization. Das et al. [2010b] propose one such design using the *key group* abstraction. Key group is a powerful yet flexible abstraction for applications to dynamically define the granules of transactional access. Any data item (or key) in the data store can be selected as part of a key group. The key groups are transient; the application can dynamically create (and dissolve) the groups. For instance, in the multi-player gaming application, a key group is created at the start of a game instance and deleted at its completion. At any instant of time, a given key is part of a single group. However, a key can participate in multiple groups whose lifetimes are temporally separated. For instance, a player can participate in a single game at any instant of time, but can be part of multiple game instances that do not temporally overlap.

Transactional guarantees are provided only for keys that are part of a group, and only during the lifetime of the group. All keys in the data store need not be part of groups. At any instant, multiple keys might not be part of any group; they conceptually form one-member groups. Every group has a *leader* selected from one of the member keys in the group; the remaining members are called the *followers*. The leader is part of the group's identity. However, from an application's perspective, the operations on the leader are no different from those supported for the followers. For ease of exposition, we will use the terms "leader" and "follower" to refer to the data items as well as the nodes where the data items are stored.

Leveraging the application's semantics that once a key group is formed, the application will execute a number of transactions during the lifetime of the group, the system can re-organize to co-locate ownership of all keys in a key group at a single node. For example, one strategy is that all followers can yield ownership to the leader. This dynamic co-location allows transactions to efficiently execute at a single node. In essence, once the application specifies a key group, the group creation phase makes an upfront investment (in terms of distributed synchronization needed to create the group) with the hope of breaking even and potentially benefitting from the efficient execution of transactions during the group's lifetime. Note that keys in a key group are co-located by choice leveraging the explicit intent expressed by the application.

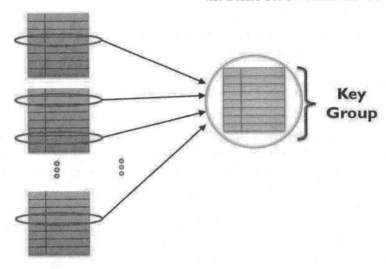

Figure 4.5: The Key Group abstraction.

Group creation is initiated by an application client (or a client) sending a *group create* request with the *group id* and the members. The group id is a combination of a unique system-generated id and the leader key. Group creation can either be *atomic* or *best effort*. Atomic group creation implies that either all members join the group or else the group is automatically deleted if one of the followers did not join. Best effort creation forms the group with whatever keys that joined the group. A data item might not join a group either if it is part of another group (since we require groups to be disjoint), or if the data item's follower node is not reachable. Das et al. [2010b] propose the *key grouping protocol* that allows safe group creating in the presence of failures. In the key grouping protocol, the leader is the *coordinator* and the followers are the *participants* or *cohorts*. The leader key can either be specified by the client or is selected by the system. The group create request is routed to the node which owns the leader key. The leader logs the member list, and sends a *Join Request* (⟨J⟩) to all the followers (i.e., each node that owns a follower key). Once the group creation phase terminates successfully, the client can issue operations on the group. When the client wants to disband the group, it initiates the group deletion phase with a *group delete* request. Figure 4.5 illustrates the key group abstraction where the keys that form the key group can be physically distributed across a number of nodes, but are logically co-located and owned by the leader. The key grouping protocol allows this dynamic ownership transfer while ensuring safety and correctness in the presence of failures.

Critical for the correctness of dynamic ownership re-organization is the protocol that manages this ownership transfer in the presence of failures. Conceptually, such transfers from followers to the leader are equivalent to the leader acquiring locks on the followers. Similarly, the reverse process is equivalent to releasing the locks. Details depend on the specific implementation, but in general, the key grouping protocol is reminiscent of the locking protocols for transaction concurrency control [Eswaran et al., 1976, Weikum and Vossen, 2001]. The difference is that in a key group, the locks are held by the key groups (i.e., the system) whereas in classical lock-based schedulers, the locks are held by the transactions.

4.2   TRANSACTION EXECUTION

In the previous section, we explained different techniques to co-locate data or ownership for data items that a transaction accesses. Once ownership is co-located, classical transaction processing techniques (discussed in § 2.3) can be used for efficient transaction execution. Different systems however differ in their choice of concurrency control and recovery techniques. On one hand, some systems (such as Cloud SQL Server, Deuteronomy [Levandoski et al., 2011], and Relational Cloud) use lock-based concurrency control techniques, such as two-phase locking (2PL). On the other hand, some other systems (such as G-Store and ElasTraS) use optimistic concurrency control (OCC). Various other systems, such as Megastore and Hyder [Bernstein et al., 2011a], use multi-version concurrency control techniques. Recovery is commonly performed by logging the operations before a transaction commits, and replaying the logged operations during recovery which are based on ARIES-style recovery algorithms [Mohan et al., 1992].

4.3   DATA STORAGE

Conceptually, efficient non-distributed transaction execution only requires that read/write access to data items accessed by a transaction be co-located at a node. The actual physical data storage can either be coupled (or co-located) or decoupled. In this section, we discuss the different alternatives for designing the storage layer.

4.3.1   COUPLED STORAGE

Coupling storage with computation has been the classical design choice for data intensive systems. The rationale is that this coupling of data and execution improves performance by eliminating the need to transfer data over a network. To further improve performance, many RDBMS engines even couple the transaction execution logic with the access methods and the recovery managers. For instance, in systems using ARIES-style recovery [Mohan et al., 1992], such as many commercial as well as open-source RDBMSs, a log sequence number is assigned to the updated pages, thus linking the database pages to the corresponding log entry.

As a side effect of co-locating ownership of data items co-accessed within a transaction, the data storage can also be coupled with the ownership. That is, the data items co-located within a transaction are also physically co-located at the server serving transactions on the partition. This design option is often used in systems that re-engineer and scale-out classical RDBMSs, such as in Cloud SQL Server or Relational Cloud, thus requiring minimal changes to the transaction and resource managers.

4.3.2   DECOUPLED STORAGE

The growing main memory sizes in commodity servers and the broader availability of low latency and high throughput data center networks allow an alternative design where the data ownership is decoupled from the physical storage of data. The rationale for such decoupling is that for most high-performance transaction processing systems, the working set is most likely cached and served from memory. For infrequent accesses to the storage layer to service cache misses, the fast networks make the difference between local disk access and remote disk access almost intangible.

On the other hand, decoupling storage from ownership and transaction processing logic has multiple benefits: (*i*) it results in a simplified design allowing the storage layer to focus on fault-tolerance while the ownership layer can guarantee higher-level guarantees such as transactional access without worrying about the need for replication; (*ii*) depending on the application's requirements it allows independent scaling of the ownership layer and the data storage layer; and (*iii*) it allows for lightweight control migration for elastic scaling and load balancing, it is enough to safely migrate only the ownership without the need to migrate data.

Two alternative decoupled storage designs have been explored in the literature. In the first class of systems, the transaction management layer controls the physical layout and format of data and the storage layer exposes an abstraction of a distributed and replicated block storage device. The alternative design is where the storage layer is self-managed, in terms of the physical data layout, format, and access paths and hides these details from the transaction management layer that interfaces with the storage layer at a logical level.

Managed Storage Layer

One alternative design option is to treat the decoupled storage layer as a distributed and replicated block storage abstraction, similar to a distributed file system such as the Google File System [Ghemawat et al., 2003] and Amazon S3. Such a design divides the design complexity between the transaction management and the storage layers. While the transaction management layer need not be aware of the physical data distribution and partitioning, or data replication, access methods, concurrency control, and recovery must be handled by the transaction management. On the other hand, the storage layer can efficiently handle replication, geo-distribution, fault-tolerance, and load balancing of data accesses and storage without possessing any knowledge of transactions or index structures.

A number of systems proposed in the literature chose this design option. Examples of such systems include ElasTraS, G-Store, and Megastore. In all these systems, ownership is co-located at a server which has the unique read/write access to the data items. To allow efficient and non-distributed transaction execution, the number of interactions with the decoupled storage layer is further reduced in these systems by caching data as well as updates locally at the node executing the transaction. These updates are asynchronously propagated to the storage layer, potentially in batches. Figure 4.6 provides a high-level architectural overview of such a system. As depicted in the figure, the storage layer is treated equivalent to a set of distributed disks managed by the transaction

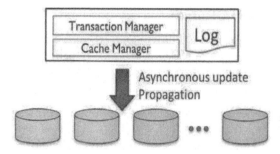

Figure 4.6: Update propagation in decoupled storage architectures.

management layer. Different systems use different approaches for update propagation depending on the logging mechanisms used during transaction execution and the recovery guarantees sought. For instance, if all updates are cached locally at the node executing the transactions, then a failure of that node might result in unavailability of the most recent updates or complete loss if the node does not recover. On the other hand, if the updates are stored in a replicated log, thus making normal operation expensive, no updates will be lost even if the transaction manager node never recovers. Such trade-offs are discussed in detail later in this chapter when we discuss the individual systems.

Self-managed Storage Layer

Another alternative design choice is to provide more autonomy to the storage layer to decide the physical layout, access methods, etc. One major benefit of making the transaction layer oblivious of the physical data layout and structures is that the transaction management layer can span different storage formats. The transaction manager operates at the granularity of logical data units. For instance, a transaction can access one data item stored in a relational store and another stored in a graph store. To allow such flexibility and physical data independence, the transaction layer and the storage layer must interface using a clean and well-defined API exposing the logical data units. Deuteronomy presents an example of such an self-managing decoupled architecture, where the storage layer (called the data component) performs its own concurrency control and recovery of the physical data structures, while the transaction layer (called the transaction component) is responsible for transaction execution, transaction-level locking, and logical recovery.

4.4   REPLICATION

Transaction execution is often orthogonal to data replication; the way a system handles data replication adds another dimension to the design space. For instance, replication can be synchronous or asynchronous; it can be primary copy-based or multi-master. Different choices provide different trade-offs in terms of consistency, availability, performance (specifically latency during normal operation), and data durability in the event of a catastrophic failure or total loss of a replica. The various trade-offs in this design space and the specific replication technique chosen by a system requires a detailed discussion which is beyond the scope of this chapter. In this section, we focus on a different aspect of replication, that is, whether replication is performed explicitly by the transaction management layer or it is implicitly handled by the data storage layer.

4.4.1 EXPLICIT REPLICATION

One choice for replicating data is to design the transaction manager to be cognizant of replication such that updates made by the transactions are explicitly replicated while transactions are executing. Such replication can either be multi-master or primary copy. A multi-master technique can be used where write transactions accessing a partition can execute on independent replicas each acting as the master. However, such multi-master replication scenarios often provide weaker consistency guarantees to allow the replicas to independently process the updates without requiring synchronization. The weaker consistency guarantees in turn result in complex application logic to tolerate data inconsistencies. On the other hand, a primary copy replication scheme executes update transactions at a primary replica; the updates (called *downstream updates*) are then replicated to the secondaries in the order they were executed at the primary. To synchronously update the secondary copies, the downstream updates can be applied to the secondaries before the transaction commits at the primary. Typically, the primary replica waits for the updates to be replicated and acknowledgments received from a quorum of secondaries instead of all the secondaries. This minimizes transaction response times and also prevents the updates from blocking when a secondary replica has failed. Such a replication mechanism is used in Cloud SQL Serve and Megastore.

One of the benefits of such a synchronous explicit primary copy-based replication techniques is high availability in case the primary replica fails. At least one of the secondary replicas has seen all updates from committed transactions, electing one of the replicas as the primary does not result in lost updates. However, a consensus-based protocol is required to orchestrate the election of the new primary; classical leader election protocols or their variants can be used to ensure correctness during such reconfiguration. Another advantage is that the replicas can process read-only transactions on fresh data while supporting weaker isolation levels, such as snapshot isolation [Berenson et al., 1995]. Furthermore, when using a quorum-based replication scheme, a minority of the replicas can be placed in a geographically distributed data center to allow disaster recovery. If a quorum of replicas are co-located within a data center, such geo-replication does not increase transaction latency. On the other hand, if all replicas are geo-distributed, such as in Megastore, it will increase transaction latency since the commit at the primary is delayed due to the higher response times involved in contacting the secondaries.

4.4.2 IMPLICIT REPLICATION

An alternative design choice for data replication is for the replication management to be transparent to the transaction execution, i.e., the transaction execution logic is unaware of any replication protocol. The updates made by a transaction can be replicated synchronously during transaction execution, or asynchronously after a transaction has completed execution. Decoupled storage architectures are amenable to such replication schemes where replication is handled transparently from transaction execution; examples of such systems include ElasTraS, G-Store, and Megastore for replication within a data center.

Implicit replication by the storage layer can be at the level of replicating the data pages (or blocks) or by replicating the transaction log. For instance, the transaction log can be stored in decoupled storage and forced at transaction commit, thus resulting in the updates being replicated synchronously by the underlying data storage layer. While such synchronous replication will increase transaction latencies, it allows the system to recover the state of transactions in the event of a failure in the transaction management layer. On the other hand, in a coupled storage architecture, asynchronous shipping of physical log entries or logical updates can be used for implicit replication. However, such asynchronous update propagation schemes can result in the loss of the tail of the log in the event of permanent failure of the server executing the transactions.

4.5   A SURVEY OF THE SYSTEMS

Thus far, this chapter has focused on abstracting the various dimensions in the design space. A transaction processing system co-locating data access to a single node can, in principle, be designed by selecting a combination of design choices from each of the design abstractions discussed. In the remainder of this chapter, we survey a set of representative systems, provide details about their architecture, and analyze how these systems combine the different abstractions into an end-to-end system.

4.5.1   G-STORE

G-Store [Das et al., 2010b] is a system that supports efficient transactional access to dynamically defined groups of keys. G-Store is layered on top of key-value stores, such as Bigtable. By supporting application-specified dynamically defined database partitioning, G-Store provides an alternative to the statically defined hierarchical schema patterns supported by Megastore and ElasTraS To allow efficient transaction execution during the lifetime of a key group, G-Store uses a protocol, called the key grouping protocol, to transfer ownership of the members of a key group to a single node that becomes the logical owner of data. Since the key groups are formed on demand, in order to minimize the cost of data movement during group formation and deletion, G-Store uses a decoupled storage architecture with the physical storage structures managed by the transaction management layer. Once a key group has been formed and ownership co-located, G-store uses optimistic concurrency control and transaction operation logging for recovery. G-Store logs a transaction's updates to a distributed storage before a transaction commits, thus allowing the system to tolerate leader failures and allowing the leader's state to be recovered from this log. Techniques such as group commit and asynchronous update propagation improve transaction throughput. G-Store relies on implicit replication in the underlying key-value store.

In its simplest form assuming reliable message delivery and no node failures, the key grouping protocol is essentially a handshake between the follower nodes and the leader node to transfer the

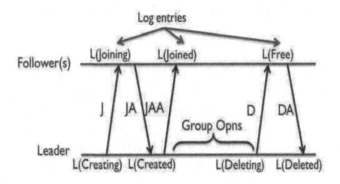

Figure 4.7: The key grouping protocol to enable logical co-location of physically distributed data.

ownership of the follower keys to the leader node. However, reliable message delivery guarantees across nodes and message failures are often expensive. For example, protocols such as TCP provide guaranteed delivery and ordering only on an active connection. However, group creation requires delivery guarantees across connections. Hence, using TCP alone will not be enough to provide message delivery guarantees in the presence of node failures or network partitions. Furthermore, in a large distributed system, node failures are also common, and ownership transfer and group management must tolerate such node failure. The key grouping protocol does not require any message delivery guarantees while ensuring correctness in the presence of node failures. The basics of the protocol are similar to a handshake often found in atomic commitment protocols, such as 2PC or TCP connection setup; additional messages, unique identifiers, and logging are added to recover from a variety of failure scenarios.

Figure 4.7 illustrates the protocol with unreliable messaging which, in the steady state, results in two additional messages, one during creation and one during deletion. During group creation, the ⟨JA⟩ message, in addition to notifying whether a key is free or part of a group, acts as an acknowledgement for the ⟨J⟩ request. On receipt of a ⟨JA⟩, the leader sends a *Join Ack Ack* ⟨JAA⟩ to the follower, the receipt of which finishes the group creation phase for that follower. This group creation phase is two phase, and is similar to the 2PC protocol for transaction commitment. The difference stems from the fact that the key grouping protocol also allows best effort group creation while 2PC would be equivalent to atomic group creation. During group dissolution, the leader sends a *Delete Request* ⟨D⟩ to the followers. On receipt of a ⟨D⟩ the follower regains ownership of the key, and then responds to the leader with a *Delete Ack* ⟨DA⟩. The receipt of ⟨DA⟩ from all the followers completes group deletion.

Group create request. On receipt of a group create request from the client, the leader verifies the request for a unique group id. The leader appends an entry to its *log* that stores the group id and the members in the group. After the log entry is *forced* (i.e., flushed to persistent storage), the leader sends a ⟨J⟩ request to each of the follower nodes. The ⟨J⟩ messages are retried until the leader receives a ⟨JA⟩ from the followers.

Join request ⟨J⟩.   On receipt of a ⟨J⟩ request the follower ascertains the freshness and uniqueness of the message. If the message is detected as a duplicate, then the follower sends a ⟨JA⟩ without appending any log entry. Otherwise, if the follower key is not part of any active group, the follower appends a log entry denoting the ownership transfer and the identity of the leader key. This ownership transfer is an update to the system's metadata, and the follower's log is the persistent storage for this information. This log entry must therefore be forced before a reply is sent. The follower's state is set to *joining*. The follower then replies with a ⟨JA⟩ message notifying its intent to yield. To deal with spurious ⟨JAA⟩ messages and eliminate the problem of phantom groups, the follower should be able to link the ⟨JAA⟩ to the corresponding ⟨JA⟩. This is achieved by using a sequence number generated by the follower called the *yield id*. A yield id is associated to a follower node and is monotonically increasing. The yield id is incremented every time a follower sends new ⟨JA⟩ and is logged along with the entry logging the ⟨J⟩ message. The yield id is copied into the ⟨JA⟩ message along with the group id. The ⟨JA⟩ message is retried until the follower receives the ⟨JAA⟩ message. This retry ensures that the phantom groups are not left undetected.

Join Ack ⟨JA⟩.   On receipt of a ⟨JA⟩ message, the leader checks the group id. If it does not match the identifiers of any of the currently active groups, then the leader sends a ⟨D⟩ message and does not log this action or retry this message. Occurrence of this event is possible when the message was a delayed message, or the follower yielded to a delayed ⟨J⟩. In either case, a ⟨D⟩ message would be sufficient and also deletes any phantom groups that might have been formed. If the group id matches a current group, then the leader sends a ⟨JAA⟩ message copying the yield id from the ⟨JA⟩ to the ⟨JAA⟩ irrespective of whether the ⟨JA⟩ is a duplicate. If this is the first ⟨JA⟩ received from that follower for this group, a log entry is appended to indicate that the follower has joined the group; however, the leader does not need to force the entry. The ⟨JAA⟩ message is never retried, and the loss of ⟨JAA⟩ messages is handled by the retries of the ⟨JA⟩ message. The receipt of ⟨JA⟩ messages from all the followers terminates the group creation phase at the leader.

Join Ack Ack ⟨JAA⟩.   On receipt of a ⟨JAA⟩ message, the follower checks the group id and yield id to determine freshness and uniqueness of the message. If the yield id in the message does not match the expected yield id, then this ⟨JAA⟩ is treated as a spurious message and is ignored. This prevents the creation of phantom groups. A delayed ⟨JAA⟩ will have a different yield id since it corresponds to an earlier group. Hence, the follower will reject it as a spurious message, thus preventing the creation of a phantom group. If the message is detected to be unique and fresh, then the follower key's state is set to *joined*. The follower node logs this event, which completes the group creation process for the follower; the log entry does not need to be forced.

Group delete request.   When the leader receives the *group delete* request from the application client, it forces a log entry for the request and initiates the process of *yielding* ownership back to the followers. The leader then sends a ⟨D⟩ message to each follower in the group. The ⟨D⟩ messages are retried until all ⟨DA⟩ messages are received. At this point, the group has been marked for deletion and the leader will reject any future transactions accessing this group.

Delete request ⟨D⟩.   When the follower receives a ⟨D⟩ request, it validates this message, and appends a log entry on successful validation of the message. This log entry signifies that it has regained ownership of the key. Since regaining ownership is a change in the system state, the log is forced after appending this entry. Irrespective of whether this ⟨D⟩ message was duplicate, stale, spurious, or valid, the follower responds with a ⟨DA⟩ message; this ⟨DA⟩ message is not retried.

Delete ack ⟨DA⟩.   On receipt of a ⟨DA⟩ message, the leader checks for the validity of the message. If this is the first message from that follower for this group, and the group id corresponds to an active group, then a log entry is appended indicating that the ownership of the data item has been successfully transferred back to the follower. Once the leader has received a ⟨DA⟩ from all the followers, the group deletion phase terminates. The log is not forced on this protocol action.

Das [2011] presents a detailed analysis to the different failure scenarios to assert the correctness of the protocol and ensure safety in the presence of different types of failures and works through the details of recovery from the different types of failure at any point during the lifetime of the group.

The key grouping protocol can handle data items joining and leaving a key group at any point during the group's lifetime. The key group abstractions can therefore be generalized. A key group is a set of data items on which an application seeks transactional access. This set can be dynamic over the lifetime of a group, thus allowing data items to join or leave the group while the group is active. Transactional guarantees are provided only to the data items that are part of the group when the transaction is executing. As earlier, new groups can be formed and groups can be deleted at any time. key groups continue to remain disjoint, i.e., no two concurrent key groups will have the same data item.

Conceptually, the key grouping protocol handles the joining and deletion of a group's data items individually; these requests are batched to improve performance. Therefore, the key grouping protocol remains unchanged to support this generalized key group abstraction. When the application requests a data item k to join an already existing group, the leader executes the creation phase of the key grouping protocol only for k joining the group. When k leaves a group, the leader ensures that k is not being accessed by an active transaction and all of k's updates have propagated to the follower node. The leader then executes the deletion phase only for k leaving the group.

In summary, G-Store uses an application-specified dynamic partitioning scheme coupled with a protocol to dynamically move ownership to limit transactions to a single node; conceptually, a key group maps to a dynamically defined partition. It uses optimistic concurrency control in a decoupled storage architecture with implicit replication managed by the storage layer.

4.5.2   ELASTRAS

ElasTraS [Das et al., 2009, 2010a] is an elastically scalable transaction processing system primarily targeting OLTP-style RDBMS-like functionality while scaling out to a cluster of commodity servers. ElasTraS views the database as a set of database partitions. The partitions form the granule of distribution, transactional access, and load balancing. For small application databases (as observed in multi-tenant platforms serving large numbers of small applications), the database can be contained entirely within a partition. However, for applications whose data requirements grow beyond a single partition, ElasTraS supports partitioning at the schema-level by co-locating data items frequently accessed together. Specifically, ElasTraS leverages hierarchical schema patterns to partition the database for large applications. ElasTraS is designed to serve thousands of *small* tenants as well as tenants that *grow big*. ElasTraS is based on a decoupled storage architecture which allows lightweight elastic scaling. The transaction manager layer manages the physical layout and indexes while the storage layer manages replication and data placement.

At the microscopic scale, ElasTraS consolidates multiple tenants within the same database process allowing effective resource sharing among small tenants. It achieves high transaction throughput by limiting tenant databases to a single process, thus obviating distributed transactions. For tenants with sporadic changes in loads, ElasTraS leverages low-cost live database migration for elastic scaling and load balancing. This allows it to aggressively consolidate tenants to a small set of nodes while still being able to scale-out on-demand.

At the macroscopic scale, ElasTraS uses loose synchronization between the nodes for coordinating operations, rigorous fault-detection and recovery algorithms to ensure safety during failures, and system models that automate load balancing and elasticity.

We explain the ElasTraS architecture in terms of the four layers shown in Figure 4.8 from bottom-up: the distributed fault-tolerant storage layer, the transaction management layer, the control layer, and the routing layer.

The Distributed Fault-tolerant Storage Layer.   The storage layer, or the Distributed Fault-tolerant Storage (DFS), is a network-addressable storage abstraction that stores the persistent data. This layer is a replicated storage manager that guarantees durable writes and strong replica consistency while ensuring high data availability in the presence of failures. Such storage abstractions are common in current data centers in the form of commercial products (such as storage area networks), scalable distributed file systems (such as the Hadoop distributed file system [HDFS]), or custom solutions (such as Amazon elastic block storage or the storage layer of Hyder). High-throughput and low-latency data center networks provide low-cost reads from the storage layer; however, strong replica consistency make writes expensive. ElasTraS minimizes the number of DFS accesses to reduce network communication and improve the overall system performance. We use a multi-version append-only storage layout that supports more concurrency for reads and considerably simplifies live migration for elastic scaling.

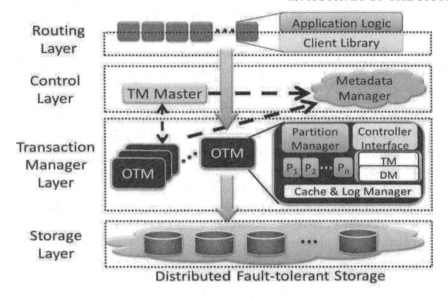

Figure 4.8: ElasTraS architecture.

Transaction Management Layer. This layer consists of a cluster of servers called Owning Transaction Managers (OTM). An OTM is analogous to the transaction manager in a classical RDBMS. Each OTM serves tens to hundreds of partitions for which it has unique ownership. The number of partitions an OTM serves depends on the overall load. The exclusive ownership of a partition allows an OTM to cache the contents of a partition without violating data consistency while limiting transaction execution within a single OTM and allowing optimizations such as *fast commit* [Weikum and Vossen, 2001]. Each partition has its own transaction manager and shared data manager. All partitions share the OTM's log manager which maintains the transactions' commit log. This sharing of the log minimizes the number of competing accesses to the shared storage while allowing further optimizations such as group commit [Bernstein and Newcomer, 2009, Weikum and Vossen, 2001]. To allow fast recovery from OTM failures and to guarantee high availability, an OTM's commit log is stored in the DFS. This allows an OTM's state to be recovered even if it fails completely.

Control Layer. This layer consists of two components: the TM Master and the Metadata Manager (MM). The TM Master monitors the status of the OTMs and maintains overall system load and usage statistics for performance modeling. The TM Master is responsible for assigning partitions to OTMs, detecting and recovering from OTM failures, and controlling elastic load balancing. On the other hand, the MM is responsible for maintaining the system state to ensure correct operation. This metadata consists of *leases* that are granted to every OTM and the TM Master, *watches*, a mechanism to notify changes to a lease's state, and (a pointer to) the *system catalog*, an authoritative mapping of a partition to the OTM currently serving the partition. Leases are uniquely granted to a server for a fixed time period and must be periodically renewed. Since the control layer stores only meta information and performs system maintenance, it is not in the data path for the clients. The state of the MM is critical for ElasTraS's operation and is replicated for high availability; the TM Master is stateless.

Routing Layer. ElasTraS dynamically assigns partitions to OTMs. Moreover, for elastic load balancing, a database partition can be migrated on-demand in a live system. The routing layer, the *ElasTraS client library* which the applications link to, hides the logic of connection management and routing, and abstracts the system's dynamics from the application clients while maintaining un-interrupted connections to the tenant databases.

Das [2011] provides more details on ElasTraS's implementation, such as transaction, log, and cache management, detecting and recovering from OTM, TM Master, and MM failures, and advanced aspects such as multi-version data and dynamic partitioning. ElasTraS effectively leverages the design principles of scalable Key-value stores and decades of research in transaction processing, thus resulting in a scale-out DBMS with transactional semantics.

In summary, ElasTraS uses the hierarchical tree schema to support a rich set of operations even when limiting transactions to a single node; for small applications, ElasTraS does not impose any restrictions on the schema or the data items accessed by a transaction. It uses optimistic concurrency control for executing transactions locally within an OTM. Storage is decoupled from transaction management and data replication is handled implicitly by the storage tier. The decoupled storage abstraction lends ElasTraS the ability to easily migrate live database partitions without incurring heavy disruption in service [Das et al., 2011].

4.5.3 CLOUD SQL SERVER

Cloud SQL Server [Bernstein et al., 2011b] adapts Microsoft's SQL Server for cloud computing workloads and scale out by partitioning the database. Cloud SQL Server is used as the back-end storage system for two large-scale web services: the Exchange Hosted Archive which is an e-mail and instant messaging repository; and SQL Azure, the relational database service offered as part of the Windows Azure storage platform.

Cloud SQL Server limits transactions to a single database partition and uses the table group schema pattern to support a rich set of transactions while avoiding two-phase commit. Each database partition is replicated. At any point in time, each database partition has one replica designated as the *primary* which executes all transactions accessing that partition. Updates from transactions executing at the primary are replicated to the secondary replicas using a custom replication scheme which is an adaptation of the primary copy replication scheme. Each database node in Cloud SQL Server is a modified SQL Server instance that serves multiple partitions within the same database process. Each node serves primaries for some database partitions and secondaries for some other partitions.

Figure 4.9 provides an overview of Cloud SQL Server's architecture. Client applications access Cloud SQL Server through a *protocol gateway* that authenticates user accesses and binds a

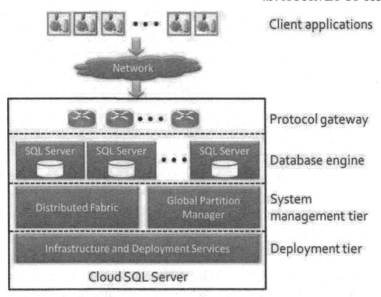

Figure 4.9: Cloud SQL Server architecture with the different major layers in the system.

user connection to a database node being accessed by the user. The gateway locates the primary for the partition being accessed and renegotiates that choice in case a failure or system-initiated reconfiguration causes the election of a new primary. Multiple user databases (or partitions) are served by a SQL Server instance running on each database node. Accesses to each partition are isolated from other partitions that are co-located with the same SQL Server process. Co-located partitions share many internal database structures and a common transaction log. High availability is provided by a highly reliable system management layer called the *distributed fabric* which implements cluster management, failure detection and recovery, and leader election. The distributed fabric uses a distributed hash table at its core to implement the system management functionalities.

The mapping of partitions to the database nodes is maintained by a highly available directory service called the *global partition manager*. The distributed fabric monitors the servers and when a failure is detected, the fabric recovers the partitions and updates the partition manager with the new location for the partition's replicas. The lowest layer in the system, called the *infrastructure and deployment services*, is responsible for provisioning and deployment tasks such as upgrading the SQL Server instances and imaging the software binaries that execute at a node.

A transaction (T) executes at the primary replica of the partition that T accesses. The primary forwards the update operations to the secondaries as the updates occur. These update operations serve as logical redo records. In case T aborts, the secondary is notified, which discards any updates corresponding to T. If T commits, then the primary assigns a commit sequence number which determines the order in which the secondaries apply updates made by T. Once a secondary completes

Row key	User.Name	Photo.Time	Photo.Tag	Photo.URL
501	John			
501,101		12:34:56	Pisa, Italy	http://img.ur/asjkh
501,102		12:56:34	Rome, Italy	http://img.ur/KGGsa
551	Jane			
551,151		11:22:33	New York, USA	http://img.ur/hgFDF
551,152		11:33:44	Santa Barbara, USA	http://img.ur/BBA7t
551,153		11:44:55	Seattle, USA	http://img.ur/kajhsl

Entity group 1 brackets rows 501, 501,101, and 501,102. Entity group 2 brackets rows 551, 551,151, 551,152, and 551,153.

Figure 4.10: Megastore's storage layout. The hierarchical structure of an entity group is leveraged to co-locate data in Bigtable.

applying T's updates, it sends an acknowledgement back to the primary. The primary writes a persistent commit record once it receives an acknowledgment from a quorum of replicas. A secondary is not required to force T's updates to the log before acknowledging the primary. That is, when T commits at the primary, a quorum of servers is guaranteed to have a copy of the commit, but is not required to have a persistent copy of the record of the commit. If the partition's replicas are unlikely to experience a correlated failure, such a replication scheme is expected to provide a satisfactory degree of fault tolerance while minimizing transaction latencies by not requiring persistence at the secondaries. In the cases where tolerance to server failures is needed, the secondaries can be required to force the commit record before acknowledging the primary. Bernstein et al. [2011b] provides further details about the replication protocol and various optimizations.

In summary, Cloud SQL Server uses a hierarchical schema pattern, the table group abstraction, to support rich functionality while limiting transactions to access a single database partition. It uses a classical RDBMS engine which relies on a two-phase locking-based concurrency control mechanism and couples storage with transaction management. Data replication is explicitly handled by the transaction management layer, thus requiring a custom quorum-based commit protocol to allow synchronous replication.

4.5.4 MEGASTORE

Megastore [Baker et al., 2011] is a scale-out data store designed to provide transactional access to small granules of data in a replicated and geographically distributed system. To scale-out, Megastore partitions data into a vast space of small databases which form the granule of transactional access. Megastore uses a hierarchical schema structure, an *entity group*, which forms the granule of ACID transactions and replication. Each entity group has its own replicated log stored in a per-replica Bigtable instance. An entity group's log is replicated synchronously to geographically distributed data centers using a fault-toleration replication protocol based on the Paxos consensus algorithm [Chandra et al., 2007, Lamport, 1998]. Such replication across data centers allows Megastore to tolerate intermittent or permanent outages at the level of a data center while providing high availability for application-level reads and writes.

Data storage and co-location. Megastore exposes the entity group abstraction where the applications can group together related data items that are accessed together, often within a single transaction. The hierarchical schema structure allows physical data co-location in the underlying Bigtable instance storing the data corresponding to an entity group. Figure 4.10 illustrates this physical co-location using the photo sharing application schema described in Figure 4.2(b). The Bigtable column name is a concatenation of the Megastore table name and the property name, allowing entities from different Megastore tables to be mapped into the same Bigtable row without collision. The Bigtable row for the root entity stores the transaction and replication metadata and the transaction log for the entity group. Storing all metadata in a single row allows Megastore to update or read the metadata using Bigtable's single row transactions API. For rows corresponding to non-root entities, the key for the Bigtable row is constructed by concatenating the key of the root entity with the key for that entity. In Figure 4.10, rows corresponding to an entity group are identified by the same background color. Depending on the size of an entity group, all of its data can be co-located within a single Bigtable table. Moreover, the contiguous key space for an entity group is also amenable to range partitioning in Bigtable.

Transaction execution within an entity group. Megastore supports ACID semantics for transactions accessing a single entity group by introducing its own library layer on top of Bigtable. Megastore relies on multi-version support in the Bigtable layer to implement multi-version concurrency control for transactions on an entity group. A timestamp-based protocol determines which values in a given Bigtable cell can be read or written. Transactions execute optimistically and are validated at completion to determine if they committed or aborted due to a conflicting concurrent transaction. A write transactions starts by reading the timestamp of the most recently committed transaction. All mutations made by a transaction are gathered into a log entry which is assigned a timestamp greater than the read timestamp of the transaction. A transaction commits if no other transaction's log entry was appended to the log since the read timestamp of the transaction. When multiple concurrent write transactions attempt to append to the log, only one transaction wins while the remaining transactions are aborted and must be restarted from the read phase. Note that this requirement serially executes transactions in an entity group, thus eliminating any concurrency of updates. The rationale for such a design is that many applications do not concurrently update an entity group. Writes from a committed transaction are applied (or made visible to other transactions) after the transaction's log record has been successfully appended.

The multi-version nature and explicit management of timestamps allows readers and writers to continue independently without blocking each other. This independence is beneficial since in many application scenarios, reads dominate writes. Further, Megastore supports reads with various isolation levels: *current*, *snapshot*, and *inconsistent*. Current and snapshot reads are supported in the

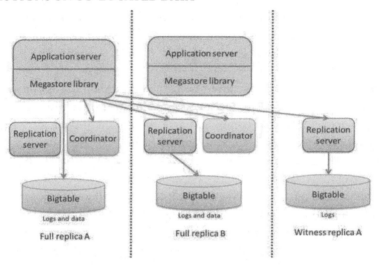

Figure 4.11: Megastore architecture layered as a library over Bigtable.

scope of an entity group. A current read is guaranteed to have seen writes of all transactions that committed before the read was issued. Snapshot reads do not provide this freshness guarantee but are guaranteed to see all writes as of a transaction in the past; the system can pick any committed transaction all of whose writes have been applied to the data store. Inconsistent reads ignore the state of the log and reads directly from the data store and hence can return updates from a partially applied transaction or updates that span multiple versions of the database. Such inconsistent reads are useful for operations that have more aggressive latency requirements.

Synchronous replication of logs using a Paxos-based protocol. Log records from an update transaction executing on an entity group are synchronously replicated to the entity group's replicas in geographically distributed data centers. The replication protocol provides a single consistent view of data stored in the underlying replicas. Figure 4.11 provides an overview of the replication architecture of Megastore, which is layered as a library over Bigtable.

Megastore adapts the Paxos protocol to minimize the number of cross-data center round trips needed to commit a write transaction. Instead of executing the prepare phase of Paxos for every transaction commit, Megastore uses a concept of implicit leaders and the prepare phase is essentially piggy-backed on the previous successful consensus round. That is, Megastore executes an independent instance of Paxos for every log position, however, the leader for each log position is a distinguished replica chosen alongside the preceding log position's consensus value. The first writer to submit a value to the leader wins the right to ask all replicas to accept that value; all other writes must fall back on two-phase Paxos. To minimize the writer to leader communication overhead, a leader is typically located in the data center from where most writes are originating.

Since the Paxos consensus protocol only requires acknowledgements from a majority of replicas, a replica might be lagging behind the most recent updates. Contacting a majority of replicas to process a read is guaranteed to return the most updated values, though at the cost of making the reads more expensive. Megastore uses a service, called a *coordinator*, local to each data center's replicas which tracks a set of entity groups whose replicas have observed all Paxos writes. For entity groups in that tracked set, the local replica has sufficient state to serve local reads. The coordinator service is an optimization to improve read latency during normal operation. However, ensuring consistency of reads in the presence of network partitions requires an additional set of protocols. Coordinators in Megastore must obtain remote leases from Chubby instances [Burrows, 2006] running in remote data centers. If a coordinator ever loses a majority of its locks from a crash or network partition, it will revert its state to a conservative default, rendering all entity groups in its purview to be out-of-date. Patterson et al. [2012] show that the Paxos implementation is correct, i.e., ensures *one-copy serializability*, but does so at the expense of executing all transactions *serially*. The basic Paxos is then enhanced to a new protocol called Paxos with Combination and Promotion (Paxos-CP) that provides true transaction concurrency while requiring the same per instance message complexity as the basic Paxos protocol.

Megastore supports three different types of replicas. A replica which serves both reads and writes is called a *full* replica. A full replica stores both the data and the logs and participates in voting during a transaction's commit. A write-only replica, called a *witness* replica, votes in Paxos rounds and stores the write-ahead log, but does not apply updates to the log to serve reads. These replicas act as tie breakers when enough full replicas are not available to form a quorum. A witness replica does not serve reads and hence does not have a coordinator, thus saving an additional round-trip when it fails to acknowledge a write. A *read-only* replica is the inverse of a voting replica. That is, a read-only replica does not vote but contains a full snapshot of data consistent as of some point in the recent past. The read-only replicas are useful to serve reads over wide geographic areas that can tolerate some staleness and do not impact write latency.

Transactions spanning multiple entity groups.   The entity group abstraction allows efficient execution of transactions that only access a single entity group. Megastore, however, also supports transactions that access multiple entity groups. Such multi-group transactions are either executed using an asynchronous fault-tolerant queue or by executing two-phase commit [Gray, 1978] on all the entity groups accessed by a transaction. Such multi-group transactions incur a higher latency compared to transactions accessing a single entity group.

In summary, Megastore uses a hierarchical schema pattern to physically co-locate an entity group's data. Transactions execute using a multi-version optimistic concurrency control technique. Storage is decoupled—-transactions execute in a library layer while data is physically stored in a logically decoupled cluster of Bigtable instances. Replication across geographically distant data centers is handled by explicitly replicating a transaction's log to a quorum of replicas before a transaction's commit is acknowledged.

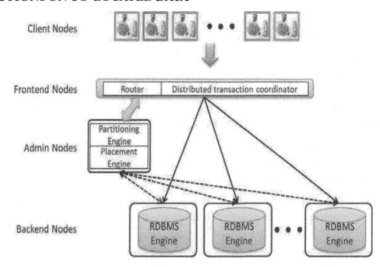

Figure 4.12: Relational Cloud Architecture.

4.5.5 RELATIONAL CLOUD

Relational Cloud [Curino et al., 2011a] presents a scale-out transaction processing architecture that relies on access-based partitioning to limit majority of transactions to access a single database partition. Figure 4.12 presents a high-level view of Relation Cloud's architecture. Similar to Cloud SQL Server, the goal is to adapt existing RDBMS engines, such as MySQL, to be able to scale-out using a shared-nothing cluster of DBMS nodes, each executing an instance of the RDBMS engine. However, Relational Cloud does allow transactions to access multiple partitions potentially distributed over a set of nodes. A subset of the front-end nodes are responsible for coordinating the execution and commit of the distributed transaction. The front-end nodes are also responsible for routing transactions based on the mapping of partitions to the nodes.

An access-driven data partitioning engine and a workload-aware partition placement engine form the administrative nodes in the system. Relational Cloud uses an access-driven partitioning scheme, Schism [Curino et al., 2010], which models data accesses as a graph, where data items form the nodes while the transactions form the edges, and uses standard off-the-shelf graph partitioning techniques to partition the graph and hence the database. The optimization goal of the partitioning algorithm is to minimize the number to edges that cross the graph cut. Edges in the graph are weighted to account for the frequency of accesses.

The partition placement algorithm monitors the workload and resource consumption of each database partition and uses these measures to determine the appropriate partitions to co-locate at a given server. The goal of the placement algorithm is to ensure high resource utilization at the backend database nodes by aggressively consolidating multiple partitions at the same node while also ensuring that enough resources are available at the node such that a tenant's performance is not

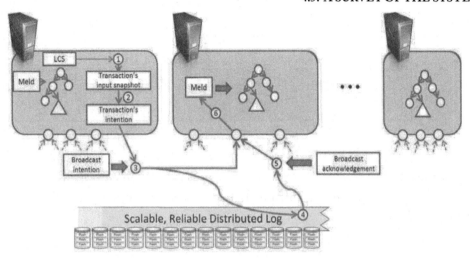

Figure 4.13: Hyder's architecture. Every node in the system executes transactions on a snapshot of the last committed state (LCS) and append's the after-image of the database (the transaction's intention) to the shared log. Nodes subsequently meld the transactions in log order to independently determine whether a transaction has committed or aborted.

affected significantly. Relational Cloud uses an integer linear programming-based solution, called Kairos [Curino et al., 2011b], to determine a good placement scheme for a given workload pattern. Kairos optimizes for short-running OLTP workloads where the working set fits easily in the database cache and disk accesses are few and far between. This requirement of infrequent disk accesses forms the basis of Kairos's model of disk IO in a consolidated setting.

In summary, Relational Cloud uses access-driven database partitioning to limit most of the transactions to access a single database partition. Within a partition, transactions use classical lock-based concurrency control and a distributed transaction coordinator uses two-phase commit for transactions accessing multiple partitions. Data storage is coupled with transaction execution.

4.5.6 HYDER

Hyder [Bernstein et al., 2011a] is an architecture that scales-out transactions without requiring applications or databases to be partitioned. This feature differentiates Hyder from other systems (such as ElasTraS, Relational Cloud, Cloud SQL Server, and G-Store) that rely on some form of partitioning for scale-out. However, similar to these systems, Hyder minimizes distributed synchronization during the execution of a transaction. In particular, a transaction that updates the database results in one distributed synchronization while read-only transactions do not incur any distributed synchronization.

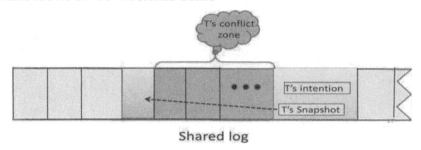

Figure 4.14: A transaction T's conflict zone that comprises transactions that executed concurrent with T and were appended to the log ahead of T. Transactions in T's conflict zone determine whether T committed or aborted.

Figure 4.13 provides an overview of Hyder's architecture. Hyder comprises a set of compute nodes that execute transactions on a shared database state. The database is stored as a log that is shared among all the compute nodes. The log *is* the database in Hyder. The database is an *immutable* tree stored in the log; the figure uses a binary search tree for illustration, though the database may be stored as a B+-tree. This immutable nature makes the database multi-version. Each node caches the tail of the log that comprises the last committed state of the database as viewed by the compute node. Transactions execute optimistically at a compute node to avoid any distributed synchronization during transaction execution.

Figure 4.13 depicts the steps in the life of a transaction. A transaction (T) executes on a snapshot of the database which corresponds to the last committed state (LCS) at the compute node (step 1). If T updates any data item, it creates an after image of the database which is called T's *intention* record (step 2); a read-only transaction executes on its LCS snapshot and commits locally without creating an intention record. A transaction executes locally at a compute node without requiring any distributed synchronization. Since the database is multi-version, the cache at a compute node is trivially coherent. A cache miss results in a read access to the log without any need for synchronization. Once T completes, its intention is broadcast to all other compute nodes and also to the log (step 3). T's intention is atomically appended to the tail of the log (step 4) which determines T's global order with respect to other concurrent transactions. Once T's position in the log is known, this position is again broadcast to all compute nodes (step 5). Each compute node (including the node that executed T) independently receives T's intention and position in the log which then processes the intentions sequentially in log order to determine T's outcome (step 6). This process of merging the intentions into the LCS in log order is called *meld* and is a deterministic function on the sequence of intentions in the log. Since every node executes meld deterministically, each node can independently determine a transaction's outcome without any need for synchronization and it is guaranteed that every node will determine the same outcome for T. Finally, the compute node where T executed notifies the outcome (commit or abort) to the application.

If multiple transactions are executing concurrently in the system, then the position of T's snapshot and T's intention is not contiguous. The intention that separates T's intention from its snapshot is called T's *conflict zone* which comprises the transactions that executed concurrently with T but were appended to the log ahead of T; Figure 4.14 illustrates a transactions conflict zone. If T conflicts with a committed transaction in its conflict zone, then T must be aborted, else T commits. The definition of conflict is contingent on the isolation level being enforced. For instance, in the case of serializable isolation, T commits only if its read and write sets do not conflict with a committed transaction in its conflict zone while in the case of snapshot isolation, T commits only if its write set does not conflict. In the case of serializable isolation, T's intention must also contain information about its read set. In principle, when processing T's intention, meld must sequentially check all the transactions in its conflict zone. However, meld in Hyder leverages the tree structure and additional metadata (in the form of structural and content version numbers) to efficiently determine T's outcome without individually processing all intentions in T's conflict zone. The efficiency of meld stems from the fact that if a node in the tree is unchanged between T's snapshot and the current LCS, then no changes were made in the subtree and hence meld does not need to analyze the subtree; details of the various optimizations is provided in Bernstein et al. [2011c].

Even though Hyder limits transaction execution to a single node, there are four bottlenecks inherent to its design that limit its peak update transaction throughput. First, all update transactions must be broadcast to all compute nodes and hence the broadcast throughput of the network connecting the compute node to the log is a bottleneck. Second, all update transactions must be appended to the shared log and hence the log append throughput is also a bottleneck. Reid and Bernstein [2010] and Balakrishnan et al. [2012] present two architectures for scalable shared logs on SSDs or flash chips which can potentially be used as the log in Hyder. Third, meld processes intentions sequentially in log order and hence is limited by the clock speed of a single processor. Finally, Hyder uses optimistic concurrency control whose peak throughput is limited by the amount of data contention. Hyder was designed to leverage various recent innovation disruptions in computer hardware and data center networks. In particular, Hyder will benefit from multi-core processors, fast data center networks, and abundant random I/O available from NAND flash. Such innovations help ease many of these bottlenecks while allowing Hyder to scale-out to tens of nodes without partitioning the database.

In summary, Hyder does not leverage partitioning of the database or the application to scale-out transaction processing. It uses a multi-version optimistic concurrency control protocol to allow transactions to execute locally at a node without requiring distributed synchronization; a transaction only synchronizes with other transactions when it appends to the shared log which imposes a global order on all the transactions. While storage is decoupled from transaction processing, Hyder uses the storage layer also as a point of synchronization, which differentiates it from other decoupled storage architectures. Hyder also has an inherent data replication mechanism where updates made by a transaction become visible to other nodes which replay all update transactions in log order.

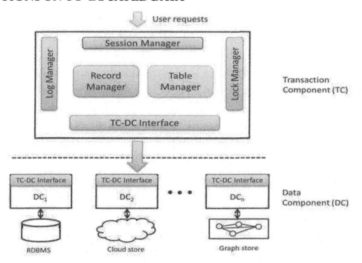

Figure 4.15: An overview of Deuteronomy architecture. The transaction component and data components are unbundled and interface through a well-defined TC-DC interface protocol.

4.5.7   DEUTERONOMY

Deuteronomy [Levandoski et al., 2011] presents a different architectural design point for supporting ACID transactions by factoring the functions of a database storage engine kernel into a transactional component (TC) and a data component (DC). A TC provides transactions via "logical" concurrency control and undo/redo recovery without being aware of the physical data layout or location of data. The DC supports a record-oriented interface with atomic operations and is responsible for physical data organization (such as data storage and indexing) and caching; the DC is oblivious of transactions. This design of Deuteronomy is different from classical storage engines where optimizations, such as multi-granularity locking or physiological logging, rely on tight coupling of transaction execution logic and the physical data layout.

Figure 4.15 presents an overview of Deuteronomy's architecture. Applications submit requests to the TC which uses a session manager to authenticate and manage these connections. The TC uses a lock manager and a log manager to logically enforce transactional concurrency control and recovery. The record manager handles the logical read and write operations for each data item and the table manager handles the data definition operations.

A TC can interact with multiple DCs using a well-defined TC-DC interaction contract [Lomet et al., 2009] that hides the details of physical data layout used by the DC. As illustrated in Figure 4.15, a TC can interface with a DC storing relational data, a DC backed by a cloud data store, and a DC storing graph data. This flexibility is one of the key advantages of Deuteronomy which eliminates the need for implementing the transaction execution logic for each type of data store. Moreover, by limiting transaction execution to a single logical entity (a TC), Deuteronomy avoids the need for a two-phase commit protocol for executing transactions spanning multiple DCs. While the TC executes the concurrency control and recovery logic, the actual data operations are passed to the appropriate DC while guaranteeing to never send conflicting concurrent operations. A TC is the unique owner of a data item, and locking within a TC ensures that conflicting operations are never concurrently sent to the DC.

The session manager within a TC does all thread management. Each incoming request is assigned a thread by the session manager. The lock manager arbitrates conflicting accesses by concurrently executing threads and may occasionally block a thread. The log manager must provide the recovery guarantees and might occasionally need to block a thread while log records are forced. Resources within the TC are all treated as logical data items, and their identification does not include physical location information. The TC manages locks without knowledge of the physical layout of the stored data; Lomet and Mokbel [2009] details mechanisms to efficiently manage such logical locking, especially for supporting predicate safety. Similarly, the log manager posts log records with resources described logically and without physical location information. These logical resources are mapped via metadata stored via the table manager to identify which DC owns the requested data. Such metadata can be added throughout the lifetime of the TC in a similar way as done with traditional database catalogs.

The DC provides both cache management and access method support, and in addition, it must fulfill the TC-DC contract, which includes control operation support, guaranteeing idempotence of operations, and recovery. A DC can be co-located at the same server as the TC or can be distributed, even over a wide area network.

In summary, Deuteronomy presents an architecture that decouples transaction execution from data storage, thus presenting an instance of decoupled storage architectures. Deuteronomy furthers this design by defining a clean interface between the TC and DC and by abstracting physical data storage information from transaction execution. Deuteronomy limits transactions to execute within a single TM. While the architecture does not mandate a technique to partition the database across different TCs, if the need arises, the partitioning techniques discussed in this chapter can potentially be used. Within a TC, Deuteronomy uses lock-based approaches for concurrency control.

CHAPTER 5

Transactions on Distributed Data

In the previous chapter, we discussed abstractions and techniques to efficiently support transactional semantics on physically or logically co-located data. In this chapter, we discuss a set of approaches that do not require co-location (neither logical nor physical) of data accessed by a transaction. Distributed synchronization is inherent to such approaches, and therefore, such approaches weaken the transactional guarantees supported to allow the system to scale-out. That is, while the techniques discussed in the previous chapter rely on some form of partitioning and limiting the data items a transaction might access, techniques discussed in this chapter restrict the guarantees provided by the transactions while allowing more flexibility on the schema or data items accessed by the transactions. For instance, some approaches relax the consistency and isolation guarantees of transactions, others limit the operations supported, while some others leverage application semantics to relax the performance requirements. In this chapter, we provide a survey of a few such approaches and highlight the trade-offs of these approaches.

5.1 DATABASE-LIKE FUNCTIONALITY ON CLOUD STORAGE

Most major cloud providers expose an abstraction of a scalable and highly available storage service, such as Amazon's Simple Storage Service (S3) and Windows Azure Storage services. Brantner et al. [2008] propose an approach to build database-like functionality on top of these storage layers while preserving the scalability and high availability features of the storage service. The key idea is to build a B-tree layer over the raw pages of data stored in the cloud storage service. Figure 5.1 provides an overview of the proposed architecture. The cloud storage service is viewed as a disk which is shared among a number of clients that access data using a record-based interface exposed by the record manager. Multiple database records are aggregated into a page which is the granule of storage and transfer from the storage layer. The page manager converts record accesses to page accesses and interacts with the storage layer. A B-tree index can be implemented on top of the page manager. The root and the intermediate nodes of the B-tree are stored as pages.

Client accesses to the database fetches the pages on-demand, which are then cached at the client. Any updates made by a client transaction are cached locally until the transaction is ready to commit. When a transaction is ready to commit, log records corresponding to the updates are appended to the storage layer. This approach is similar to classical redo-based recovery. Figure 5.2

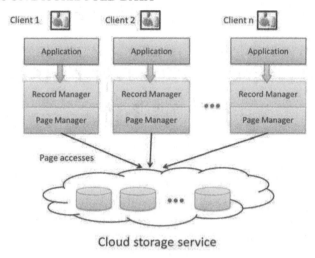

Figure 5.1: Architecture of a database system built on Amazon's simple storage service (S3).

illustrates the basic commit and checkpointing protocol. Committing a client's updates is a two-step process.

In the first step, the client generates log records for all the updates made by the transaction. These log records are appended to a queue called the *pending updates* (PU) queue. Each PU queue is responsible for storing the updates corresponding to a fragment of the database. For instance, all the internal nodes in a B-tree index can be mapped to one PU queue while the leaf nodes each have their individual PU queue. Many cloud providers also support a scalable and highly available queuing service, such as Amazon's Simple Queuing Service (SQS) or Microsoft's Windows Azure Queue Storage Service. The PU queues can be implemented using such a queuing service. The log records contain enough information to guarantee idempotence, i.e., an update in a log record is applied at most once.

In the second step of the commit protocol, the log records are applied to the pages in the storage layer, a step similar to checkpointing in classical DBMSs. Checkpoints can be carried out at any time and by any node (or client) of the system. A checkpoint strategy determines when and by whom a checkpoint is carried out. A client performing a checkpoint must ensure that no other client is concurrently performing a checkpoint on the PU queue. This synchronization is achieved using the *lock queue* corresponding to the PU queue. The lock queue is a special queue that consists of a single message. When a client wants to perform a checkpoint, it removes this message from the queue. If multiple clients concurrently try to remove the message from the queue, only one of them will succeed. The client that successfully removes the message gets the lock and will proceed with the checkpoint. Once the client completes checkpointing, it puts the message back to the lock queue. To deal with the failure of a checkpointing client, mechanisms such as timed removal can be used

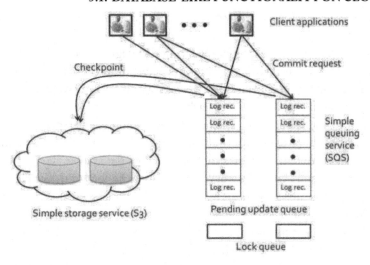

Figure 5.2: The commit and checkpointing protocol.

where the message re-appears in the lock queue so that another client can continue checkpointing starting from where the previous failed client had failed. Checkpointing the internal nodes of the B-tree requires some additional handling [Brantner et al., 2008].

The simple checkpointing protocol does not guarantee atomicity. That is, if a client failed after appending a subset of its log records to the PU queue, the checkpointing protocol does not reject such partial updates. Classical RDBMSs achieve atomicity by appending a commit record at the end of a transaction that signifies that the transaction has committed and all its updates have been logged ahead of this commit record. During recovery, any transaction missing the commit record is aborted and its updates are undone. An approach similar to this can be used in this architecture by associating an *atomic* queue with every client. The client first appends all log records to the atomic queue. Once all the records have been appended, the client appends the commit record to the atomic queue. The commit record contains the transaction id and the number of log records that the transaction created. Subsequently, the client executes the two phases of the commit protocol as described earlier. The absence of a commit record in the atomic queue implies that a transaction has failed and must be aborted.

It is important to note that since the data pages are distributed, providing the ACID transactional properties requires distributed synchronization and hence is expensive. For instance, guaranteeing atomicity of transactions requires an additional round to messages between the client and the storage layer (via the atomic queue). Guaranteeing transaction isolation and stronger forms of consistency requires even more synchronization [Brantner et al., 2008]. Therefore, while the distributed nature of data allows higher scalability, transactional guarantees become expensive and such an architecture can only support weaker guarantees while incurring reasonable overheads due to synchronization.

Since different levels of consistency incur different degrees of distributed synchronization and hence different costs, one can envision a framework where different data items have different consistency requirements, and the clients pay for stronger consistency only when such stronger guarantees are required for application correctness. Kraska et al. [2009] propose a mechanism for *consistency rationing* that allows the application designers to specify consistency guarantees on data items and allows such guarantees to be dynamically altered automatically at runtime. The adaptation is driven by a cost model and different strategies that dictate how the system should behave. The price of consistency can be measured by the number of messages exchanged or the synchronization overhead. Similarly, the price of inconsistency can be measured by the percentage of incorrect operations as a result of the lower consistency guarantees and the corresponding penalties that such inconsistent operations resulted. Using this knowledge of price and certain policies, the consistency guarantees provided for certain data items can be changed dynamically.

The key idea is to divide all data items into three categories (A, B, and C) and use different sets of protocols for processing operations on data items belonging to each category. Category A contains data items where consistency is critical and a violation can result in large penalties. Category C contains data items that are more amenable to inconsistencies, i.e., where temporary inconsistencies are acceptable. Category B consists of data items whose consistency requirements vary over time. By dynamically changing the protocols used to execute operations accessing B-type data items, the system can adapt the cost of each operation and pay for high consistency only when it is needed.

For instance, consider an e-commerce retailer. In such an application, customer profiles, financial information, the transactions corresponding to purchases and deliveries, etc., form critical information which is important for the e-tailer and calls for stringent consistency guarantees. Such types of data will form Category A types. On the other hand, other types of data, such as customer reviews of products, buying preferences, and product recommendations for a given customer profile can tolerate some temporary inconsistencies or staleness. Hence, such types of data can be categorized as type C. Finally, the consistency guarantees on product inventory might vary with time. For instance, when large quantities of a product are in stock, temporary inconsistencies in the actual quantity in stock might be acceptable. However, when only a few items are in stock, the exact count might be important to ascertain which customer gets that last item remaining in inventory and which customer's order processing will fail. Such types of data form category B data.

Since the consistency guarantees are defined at the granularity of individual data items, for transactions that access data items from different categories, operations on every record are executed based on the category that data item belongs to. Therefore, the consistency guarantee of the overall transaction will be bounded by the weakest consistency guarantee corresponding to a data item accessed by the transaction.

Data items in category B switch between strong consistency and weak consistency at run time. Different policies can be used to govern when such a switch happens. One policy is to dynamically track the probability of conflict for a given data item and switch to higher consistency guarantees when the probability is higher than a specified threshold. Another policy can be to switch the consistency guarantees based on time, i.e., running at a weak consistency level until a given point in time when consistency switches to a stronger level. Yet another policy can be to switch the consistency guarantees when the value corresponding to the data item falls below a specific threshold. For instance, considering the example of the e-tailer, weaker consistency is used when large quantities of a product is in stock and when the stock drops below a threshold, such as 100, then switch to a stronger consistency guarantee, and vice versa. Kraska et al. [2009] provide some mathematical models on how some of these policies, and many other variants, can be implemented in an operational system and how the consistency guarantees can be adapted dynamically.

Note that such dynamic adaptation of consistency guarantees is motivated by the fact the higher consistency comes at a higher cost. While this difference in cost might be significant in some systems, specifically where distributed synchronization is required for supporting stronger consistency. In various other systems, such as the ones where data or ownership is co-located (Chapter 4), where the cost to support stronger levels of consistency might not be significantly higher, the applicability of the proposed rationing approach is unclear. Further, in many operational systems, the cost of inconsistency and the cost to support higher consistency might not be directly comparable. Application of consistency rationing in such scenarios will require further analysis, potentially on a case-by-case basis.

5.2 TRANSACTIONAL SUPPORT FOR GEO-REPLICATED DATA

Many large applications are accessed by users that are geographically distributed. Geographic replication is important to support low latency data accesses for such applications, thus requiring data to be geographically distributed. Providing transactional access to such distributed data entails distributed transactions. Sovran et al. [2011] present a new isolation level, called *Parallel Snapshot Isolation (PSI)* to support efficient transactional accesses in such scenarios.

Supporting transactions with serializable isolation will be prohibitively expensive in such geo-replicated data stores. Even snapshot isolation (SI), which requires a total order on all update transactions, requires that every update transaction must synchronize even if they are executing in different data centers and writing to independent sets of data items. PSI is strictly weaker than SI in the sense that PSI does not enforce a global order among all update transactions. Specifically, if we consider the data store to be distributed among a number of data centers, nodes within a data center observe transactions according to a consistent snapshot and a common ordering of the transactions. However, PSI only enforces causal ordering between hosts in different data centers, thus allowing transactions to be replicated asynchronously and avoiding expensive cross-data center synchronization for every commit. Note that PSI still ensures that if two or more concurrent transactions are writing to the same data item, then only one of them commits. PSI does not necessarily enforce a total order on update transactions that do not make conflicting updates. To prevent such conflicts,

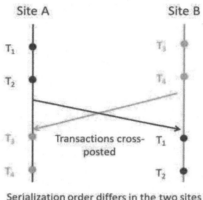

Figure 5.3: An illustration of ordering of transactions in parallel snapshot isolation.

every data item designates a *preferred site* where object can be written to without requiring any cross-data center synchronization. Moreover, PSI also preserves a causal ordering between transactions, i.e., if a transaction T_1 causally precedes transaction T_2, then this ordering is preserved across all sites.

One of the key differences between SI and PSI is that PSI allows different commit orderings of transactions on different sites. Consider the example shown in Figure 5.3 where site A executes transactions T_1 and T_2 and site B executes transactions T_3, T_4. PSI allows site A to first incorporate the updates of just T_1, T_2 and later T_3 and T_4. On the other hand, site B first incorporates updates from transactions T_3 and T_4 followed by transaction T_1 and T_2. Such different ordering of update transactions on different sites is not allowed in SI but is possible in PSI. This flexibility of lazily determining the order of non-conflicting transactions allows the system to asynchronously replicate transactions. As shown in Figure 5.3, site A can commit transactions T_1 and T_2 without coordinating with site B and then asynchronously propagates these updates after the transactions have committed at site A.

Sovran et al. [2011] implement PSI in Walter, a geographically distributed and replicated key-value store that supports transactions. Walter uses the notion of preferred sites and commutative operations, such as a conflict-free counting set (*cset*), to minimize the synchronization needed to ensure that two concurrent transactions do not make a conflicting write. The preferred site of a data item stores the authoritative version of the data items and has the exclusive right to perform local updates on the data item. A transaction executing at site A can commit locally (called a *fast commit*) without the need to synchronize with any other site if it only updated data items for which site A is the preferred site or it updates items that belong to cset. Operations on cset are commutative and hence the relative ordering between such operation is irrelevant, i.e., irrespective of the order in which the operations will be applied, the final outcome is the same after all operations have been applied; Shapiro et al. [2011] present a number of such conflict-free replicated data types which are potentially useful, minimizing synchronization in replicated systems.

On the other hand, if a transaction accesses a data item for which the local site is not the preferred site, then it must synchronize with the preferred site to synchronize the write and ensure that no concurrent transaction makes a conflicting write. Such synchronization is achieved by executing a *slow commit* protocol similar to 2PC where participants are the preferred sites of all written objects, and a server at the site executing the transaction as the coordinator. In the first phase, the coordinator asks each preferred site to vote for commit based on whether the objects modified by the transaction are unmodified and not locked. If an object has been modified at the local site, then it implies that a concurrent transaction has committed a write. On the other hand, if an item is locked, this implies that a local fast commit or a concurrent slow commit is in progress. In either case, the current transaction seeking to commit must abort and hence the participant responds with a no. If both checks pass, then the participant locks the data item(s) and responds with a yes. The coordinator commits the transaction in the second phase if all the participants responded with a yes. The transaction is otherwise aborted. Similar to any 2PC protocol, this slow commit protocol can potentially result in blocking due to coordinator failure in the second phase of the protocol. Sovran et al. [2011] present a detailed analysis of the protocol for various failure scenarios as well as a detailed specification for PSI.

5.3   INCREMENTAL UPDATE PROCESSING USING DISTRIBUTED TRANSACTIONS

In Chapter 4, we provided examples of many applications that are amenable to data partitioning and co-location. However, such partitioning might not be possible in various other applications. Consider the case of an inverted index of web pages, which is a basic structure used by most search engines. A web crawler continually scans the web for new pages or for changes to existing pages. Incrementally updating the web index as new pages or updates are crawled is desirable for freshness of results served by the search engine. Processing a crawled web page might result in updates to different parts of the index. And considering the scale of the web, the index is potentially distributed over thousands of servers. Therefore, such updates will invariably access multiple nodes and performing them as a transaction will make distributed transactions inevitable.

Percolator [Peng and Dabek, 2010] provides two main abstractions for processing such incremental updates at large scale. It provides cross-row, cross-table transactions with ACID snapshot isolation semantics [Berenson et al., 1995]. Furthermore, Percolator supports the notion of *observers* that allow organizing incremental computation. Percolator is built as a layer on top of Bigtable, a scalable and distributed key-value store. Percolator relies on a *timestamp oracle* which provides strictly increasing timestamps critical for correctness of the snapshot isolation protocol that isolates concurrent update transactions.

Percolator relies on the multi-versioned storage functionality to Bigtable to implement snapshot isolation; each version has a unique timestamp associated with it. This ensures that writes do not block any reads since an update will result in a newer version while reads can continue using the older versions. Since snapshot isolation must prevent concurrent writes to the same data items, writers to a data item must be serialized. Percolator uses locks, stored in special in-memory columns of the rows being updated, to synchronize such updates.

A transaction begins execution by obtaining a start timestamp from the timestamp oracle. This start timestamp defines the consistent snapshot that the read operations of this transaction will read from. Updates made by a transaction are buffered during execution and will be applied when the transaction is ready to commit. Since a transaction can update data items distributed over a set of nodes, atomically committing the updates requires a two-phase commit coordinated by the client. At each node, an update to a data item is executed using the row transaction API of Bigtable. In the first phase of commit (*prewrite*), the transaction tries to acquire a lock on each row it plans to update. Once a lock is obtained, the row's version is checked to determine if a concurrent writer has successfully committed, in which case the current transaction must abort to avoid a write-write conflict which is not admitted by snapshot isolation. If no conflict is detected, then the update is applied to the row while the transaction continues to hold the lock on the data items. If the transaction did not conflict on any of the rows, it may commit and proceed to the second phase. The beginning of the second phase is marked by the client obtaining a commit timestamp from the timestamp oracle. Then, at each row, the client releases its lock and makes its write visible to readers by replacing the lock with a write record. The write record indicates to the readers that the most recent version corresponds to updates made by a committed transaction. The write record also stores a pointer to the previous version. As soon as one of these writes have succeeded, the transaction must commit since it has made a write visible to readers. This two-phase commit protocol differs from the classical 2PC protocol in that the coordinator does not have a local log where it writes the outcome of a transaction. This prevents the system from blocking on coordinator failure which might be common in the case of Percolator where the clients act as coordinators.

Due to the distributed nature of the transactions, a transaction can obtain a start timestamp that exceeds the commit timestamp of a transaction that is still in the second phase of the commit protocol. Therefore, a read operation first checks for a lock in the timestamp range [0, start timestamp], which corresponds to the range of timestamps visible in the transaction's snapshot. The presence of a lock implies that another transaction is concurrently writing this cell. Hence, the reading transaction must wait until the write completes and the lock is released. In the absence of a conflicting lock, the read request returns the most recent write record.

Typical to any distributed commit protocol, the failure of the coordinator stalls execution of the transaction and potentially some other concurrent transactions that are blocked due to locks acquired by the now stalled transaction. However, all persistent information in Percolator is maintained within Bigtable, a client's failure does not indefinitely block transactions, and a subsequent cleanup can unblock some of these resources. Percolator takes a lazy approach to cleanup: when a transaction T_A encounters a conflicting lock left behind by transaction T_B, T_A may determine that T_B has failed and erases its locks. To avoid a race between a clean-up transaction and a slow but still-not-failed transaction, Percolator designates one row in every transaction as a synchronization point for any commit or cleanup operations. This row's lock is called the primary lock.

If the client crashes during the second phase of a commit, a transaction will be past the commit point (it has written at least one write record) but will still have locks outstanding. An approach similar to clean-up can be used to roll-forward the updates made by this failed transaction. A transaction that encounters a lock can distinguish between the two cases by inspecting the primary lock: if the primary lock has been replaced by a write record, the transaction which wrote the lock must have committed and the lock must be rolled forward. To roll forward, the stranded lock is replaced with a write record as the original transaction would have done. Peng and Dabek [2010] provide many more details of the protocol and further optimizations.

While Percolator provides an interesting mechanism for incremental processing of updates, it must be noted that this design benefits from certain application characteristics. For instance, an update transaction might be blocked if the client coordinating its commit fails, and it can block some other subsequent transactions. Since Percolator targets the scenario where atomicity and isolation are more important than low latency of update transactions, such blocked transactions do not adversely affect the performance targets. Furthermore, implementing serializable isolation in such a setting will considerably increase the synchronization costs and the impact of stalled transactions due to a failed client. Percolator shows that for certain applications, where latency of update transactions is not the primary focus, distributed transactions can be scaled out to thousands of servers while providing acceptable levels of isolation.

5.4 SCALABLE DISTRIBUTED SYNCHRONIZATION USING MINITRANSACTIONS

Many applications do not require the full flexibility supported by transactions. Rather, such applications might just require sharing state in a fault-tolerant, scalable, and consistent manner. Sinfonia [Aguilera et al., 2007] presents the *minitransaction* primitive for such applications to atomically access and conditionally modify data at multiple nodes. Examples of such applications include a file system distributed over a cluster of servers or a group communication service.

One of the primary benefits of the minitransaction primitive is to hide the complexities of the distributed nature of data and failures, which are a norm in large distributed systems. While providing many of the guarantees that are similar to classical database transactions, a minitransaction limits the set of supported operations to ensure that the synchronization and message passing overhead does not become significant enough to hinder scalability which is a primary requirement. In particular, the minitransaction primitive limits the set of supported operations to those that can be executed within the 2PC protocol, which is executed to atomically commit the distributed operation. This allows Sinfonia to limit the number of network round trips to two per minitransaction which is a strict limit when compared to classical distributed transactions where the number of round trips during transaction execution is not bounded, only the commit is bounded to two round trips. Moreover, minitransactions allow users to batch together updates, which eliminates multiple network round-trips.

Sinfonia consists of a set of nodes (called memory nodes) and a user library that runs at application nodes. Memory nodes store and serve application data that can either be in RAM or on stable storage according to application needs. The user library implements mechanisms to manipulate data at memory nodes using the minitransaction primitive. The memory nodes and application nodes are logically separate, though they might be physically co-located at the same server.

Minitransactions allow an application to update data in multiple memory nodes while ensuring atomicity, consistency, isolation, and (if wanted) durability. The key idea is to support a set of operations where either the last action does not affect the coordinator's decision to abort or commit the transaction, or it is known upfront how the outcome will affect the decision. In either case, such an action can be piggy-backed onto the first phase of the two-phase commit executed to commit the transaction. Every participant performs the operation received in the first phase and independently determines success or failure and can respond to the coordinator accordingly. For instance, if the write operation on a data item is not preceded by a read of the data item (i.e., the operation is a *blind write*), then the participant can execute the write and respond to the coordinator. In case a write operation is contingent on a condition to be satisfied (i.e., a *conditional write*), the participant can locally determine if the condition for the write is satisfied, apply the write if the condition is satisfied, and respond to the coordinator based on the outcome of the condition. The coordinator collects the vote from all the participants and then executes the second phase of the commit protocol which commits the transaction if all the participants responded with positively.

Stated formally, a minitransaction comprises a set of compare items, a set of read items, and a set of write items that are chosen before the minitransaction starts executing. During execution, a minitransaction compares the locations in the compare items against the data in the compare items and if all comparisons succeed (or if some compare items are absent), it returns the values in the read items and writes to the locations in the write items. A minitransaction aborts if any of the comparisons fail. Therefore, the compare items control whether the minitransaction commits or aborts, while the read and write items determine what data the minitransaction returns and updates respectively.

Examples of minitransactions include the following:

Swap: A read item returns the old value and a write item replaces it.

Compare-and-swap: A compare item compares the current value against a constant; if equal, a write item replaces it.

Atomic read of many data: Done with multiple read items.

Acquire a lease: A compare item checks if a location is set to 0; if so, a write item sets it to the (non-zero) id of the leaseholder and another write item sets the time of lease.

Acquire multiple leases atomically: Same as above, except that there are multiple compare items and write items. Note that each lease can be in a different memory node.

Change data if lease is held: A compare item checks that a lease is held and, if so, write items update data.

A common use of the minitransactions primitive is to use compare items to validate data and, if data are valid, use write items to apply some changes to the same or different data. Aguilera et al. [2007] show how the minitransaction primitive can be used to implement two scalable and distributed applications: a distributed file system and a group communication service.

Sinfonia's use of 2PC for executing minitransactions differs from the classical 2PC protocol by eliminating the coordinator log, thus eliminating indefinite blocking when the clients (acting as the coordinator) fails. Rather, Sinfonia blocks on participant failures. A *recovery coordinator* is responsible for cleaning up the state of any transaction left in the undecided state due to the coordinator failing before commit. The recovery coordinator effectively re-executes the two-phase commit with the difference that it requests the participants to abort the transaction. If none of the participants have committed the transaction, then the transaction can be aborted. However, if one or more participants committed the transaction before the coordinator failed, then this recovery coordinator commits the transaction. Aguilera et al. [2007] present the detailed minitransaction protocol and a case analysis of the different failure and recovery scenarios.

5.5 DISCUSSION

In this chapter, we discussed a number of techniques to support transactional guarantees on distributed data. In such scenarios, distributed synchronization is inevitable. In order to limit distributed synchronization, these approaches either resort to weaker isolation and consistency guarantees or restrict the types of operations that can be executed as a transaction. Brantner et al. [2008] propose an approach that provides atomicity and isolation levels such as read committed; Walter uses Parallel Snapshot Isolation (a weaker form of snapshot isolation) for geo-replicated data; Percolator leverages application semantics to relax the performance requirements as well as the isolation guarantees sought; and Sinfonia exposes the minitransaction primitive which limits transactions to only six operation types.

Various other systems and approaches have also been proposed in literature that make many design choices similar to the systems discussed in this paper. For instance, Vo et al. [2010] present a design of a system, called ecStore, that allows transactions on distributed data while providing weaker forms of isolation. Thomson et al. [2012] present a deterministic scheduling and sequencing layer, called Calvin, that deterministically schedules execution of distributed transactions which obviates the two-phase commit protocol needed for atomic commitment of distributed transactions. The key idea is to eliminate non-determinism from the transactions. A sequencer determines an execution order for the transactions and the storage nodes execute the transactions in this pre-determined order.

Different from these systems that support a transaction-like abstraction, Lloyd et al. [2011] present a weaker form of consistency, called *causal+* consistency, for preserving causality among operations in a geographically distributed and replicated database system. In systems that do not have transactional support, such as key-value stores, very little consistency guarantees are provided for operations that access multiple data items. Lloyd et al. [2011] present a technique to explicitly track causal dependencies between operations, delay operations in cases where a causally preceding update hasn't been applied, and use a convergence mechanism in case divergent versions of the same data item are detected.

Finally, Google recently published about its globally distributed database called Spanner [Corbett et al., 2012]. Spanner's *universe* spans multiple geographically distributed data centers distributed across the globe. A radical departure from some of the existing large-scale systems, Spnanner supports distributed transactions and a relational-like data model. Spanner's data model is relational with nesting using Google's protocol buffers. One of the first customers using Spanner was Google's advertisements database F1 [Shute et al., 2012] for storing and serving data that drives Google's advertisement businesses. One of the major innovations that enables Spanner is the *True Time* API which exposes synchronized timestamps as a first-class API while also providing a bound on the expected error in the time measurements. It is well known that a robust measure of time in a large geographically distributed system is extremely challenging. True time achieves this synchronization by using custom hardware, such as global positioning system (GPS) receivers and high-precision atomic clocks, at designated time servers available within each data center. The time servers use readings from the GPS receiver and the atomic clocks and a well-known protocol [Marzullo and Owicki, 1983] to synchronize time. GPS receivers and atomic clocks have independent failure modes, thus providing high availability to the timing service which forms a critical component in the infrastructure. The data servers in Spanner contact multiple local time servers to obtain an estimate of the current time and an error bound. Once a globally synchronized timestamp is known, classical timestamp-based concurrency control techniques are used for transaction execution while leveraging the underlying multi-version data store to serve snapshot reads.

CHAPTER 6

Multi-tenant Database Systems

In the previous chapters of this book, we focused on large-scale applications that needed their databases to scale to thousands of transactions per seconds and span tens of thousands of servers within a data center or across geographically separated data centers. In this chapter, we shift our focus to another class of applications typically observed in a cloud platform, namely applications whose database and usage footprints are *small*. Such applications are typically observed in Software-as-a-Service (*SaaS*) solutions such as Salesforce.com or Microsoft Dynamics CRM (customer relationship management), and in applications deployed in various Platform-as-a-Service (*PaaS*) providers such as Google AppEngine and Microsoft Window Azure. Such SaaS and PaaS cloud infrastructures typically serve hundreds of thousands of small applications (called *tenants*). Dedicating a DBMS server for each tenant is often wasteful since the individual tenants' resource requirements are often small. In order to reduce the total cost of operation, cloud providers typically share resources among the tenants, a model referred to as *multi-tenancy*. Multi-tenancy is possible in all tiers of the cloud software stack: the web/application tier, the caching tier, and the database tier (refer to Figure 1.1 for a simplified view of the cloud software stack). This chapter focuses on multi-tenancy in the database tier. Sharing the underlying data management infrastructure among a pool of tenants allows efficient use of resources and lowers the overall cost of serving applications.

In addition to the sheer scale of the number of applications deployed, these small applications deployed in cloud platforms are often characterized by high variance in popularity, unpredictable load characteristics, flash crowds, and varying resource requirements. As a result, Cloud service providers hosting these applications face unprecedented challenges in serving these applications and managing their data. Such challenges include management of large DBMS installations supporting *thousands of tenants*, *tolerating failures*, *dynamic partitioning of databases*, *elastic load balancing* for effective resource utilization and cost optimization.

The concept of a multi-tenant database has been predominantly used in the context of Software as a Service (SaaS). The Salesforce.com model [Weissman and Bobrowski, 2009] is often cited as a canonical example of this service paradigm. However, it is also interesting to study the various other models of multi-tenancy in the database tier [Jacobs and Aulbach, 2007, Reinwald, 2010] and their interplay with resource sharing in the various cloud paradigms. A thorough understanding of these models of multi-tenancy is crucial for designing effective database management system (DBMS) targeting different application domains.

Many large enterprises, in addition to public cloud providers, often host a vast number of databases to serve a variety of disjoint projects or teams. These enterprises can leverage a multi-tenant cloud platform to consolidate the number of servers dedicated to database hosting. Curino et al. demonstrated, with the consolidation engine Kairos, that the number of database nodes can be consolidated by a factor between 5.5:1 and 17:1 [Curino et al., 2011b]. Large multi-tenant databases are therefore an integral part of the infrastructure that serves such large numbers of small applications.

In this chapter, we provide a summary of multiple efforts in designing large multi-tenant database systems targeted to serve a large number of small applications typically encountered in a DBMS for a PaaS paradigm or enterprise environment. We concentrate on system-level issues related to enabling a multi-tenant DBMS for a broader class of systems. We specifically focus on elastic load balancing which ensures high resource utilization and lowers operational costs, live migration of a database as a primitive for elasticity, and some preliminary efforts for autonomic control of multi-tenant databases hosted in the cloud. Note that some of the scale-out transaction processing systems, such as ElasTraS, Relational Cloud, Megastore, and Cloud SQL Server, were also designed with native support for multi-tenancy.

6.1 MULTI-TENANCY MODELS

Multi-tenancy in the database tier can be achieved by sharing at various levels of abstraction. Sharing resources at different levels of abstraction and distinct isolation levels results in different multi-tenancy models in the database tier.[1] Three multi-tenancy models have been explored in the past [Jacobs and Aulbach, 2007]: *shared hardware*, *shared process*, and *shared table*. SaaS providers, such as Salesforce.com, typically use the shared table model. The shared process model is used in a number of database systems for the cloud, such as Relational Cloud, Cloud SQL Server, and Elas-TraS. Soror et al. [2008] and Xiong et al. [2011] propose systems using the *shared hardware* model. Figure 6.1 depicts the three multi-tenancy models and the level of sharing. A thorough understanding of these models of multi-tenancy is crucial for understanding the design space of multi-tenant DBMSs. In this section, we discuss these multi-tenancy models and analyze their trade-offs.

6.1.1 SHARED HARDWARE

In the shared hardware model, tenant databases only share the server hardware resources. Such sharing can be achieved by using a virtual machine (VM) to host each tenant's database. Each tenant is assigned its own VM and an exclusive database process that serves the tenant's database. The VMs provide an abstraction as if the tenant's database was being hosted on its own hardware. This multi-tenancy model is predominantly used in Infrastructure-as-a-Service (*IaaS*) cloud providers such as Amazon web services. In an IaaS cloud, the primary supported abstraction is a VM. Each tenant obtains a VM where its DBMS is hosted; multiple VMs will potentially be co-located at the same server. While this model offers strong security isolation among tenants, it comes at the cost of increased overhead due to redundant components and a lack of coordination using limited machine resources in a non-optimal way. Consider the instance of disk sharing among the tenants. A VM

---

[1]The term isolation in the context of multi-tenancy refers to performance isolation, resource isolation, or access-control isolation among tenants sharing the same multi-tenant DBMS. This is different from the use of isolation in the context of concurrent transactions.

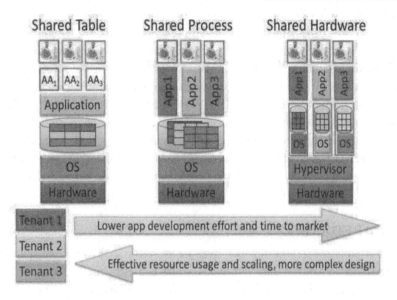

Figure 6.1: The different multi-tenancy models and their associated trade-offs.

provides an abstraction of a virtualized disk that might be shared by multiple VMs co-located on the same node. The co-located database processes make un-coordinated accesses to the disk. This results in high contention for the disk that can considerably impact performance in a consolidated setting. A recent experimental study by Curino et al. [2011b] shows that this performance overhead can be up to an order of magnitude. This model might therefore be useful when only a small number of tenants are executing at any server. As the number of tenants that need to be consolidated on the same server increases, the overheads associated with this model dominates. The advantages of this model, however, is that multi-tenancy can be supported without any changes in the database layer.

6.1.2 SHARED PROCESS

In this model, tenants share resources within a single database process running at each server. This sharing can happen at various isolation levels—from sharing only some database resources such as the logging infrastructure to sharing all resources such as the buffer pool, transaction manager, etc. This model allows for effective resource sharing between the tenants while allowing the DBMS to intelligently manage some critical resources such as the disk bandwidth. This will allow more tenants to be consolidated at a single server while ensuring good performance. This multi-tenancy model is typically observed on PaaS cloud providers such as Microsoft SQL Azure, Google Megastore, etc.

Tenants are typically only provided security isolation. Since most traditional DBMSs were not designed for such native support of multi-tenancy, today's DBMSs provide minimal or no resource or performance isolation among tenants. The advantage of this model is that it allows more effective sharing of some of the critical physical resources such as I/O and main memory while at the same time ensuring a level of isolation of user data in separate tables. Most commercial DBMS solutions can support this model easily, since all of them have a concept of supporting multiple databases in a single DBMS instance.[2] However, this support is static in the sense that it does not support the notion of elasticity that would allow dynamic migration of databases hosted at one DBMS instance to move to another DBMS. Also, the design flexibility was intended for hosting a handful of databases. Anecdotal evidence suggests that DBMSs become sluggish when they are used to host a large number of tenant databases especially when workload spikes. Manual intervention becomes necessary to deal with such performance crises. Narasayya et al. [2013] present an abstraction, called SQLVM, to enable performance and resource isolation among tenants sharing the same DBMS process.

6.1.3 SHARED TABLE

In the shared table model, the tenants' data are stored in a shared table called the *heap table*. To support flexibility in schema and data types across the different tenants, the heap table does not contain the tenant's schema or column information. Additional meta-data structures, such as *pivot tables* [Aulbach et al., 2008, Weissman and Bobrowski, 2009], provide richer database functionality such as the relational schema, indexing, key constraints, etc. The reliance on consolidated and specialized pivot and heap tables implies re-architecting the query processing and execution functionality, in addition to performance implications since the tenants' resources are not isolated, and workloads from independent tenants contend for the shared resources. Additionally, the shared table model requires that all tenants reside on the same database engine and release (or version). This limits specialized database functionality, such as spatial or object based, and requires that all tenants use a limited subset of functionality. This multi-tenancy model is ideal when multiple tenants have similar schema and access patterns with minimal customizations, thus providing effective sharing of resources. Such similarity is observed in SaaS where a generic application tenant is customized to meet specific customer requirements.

6.1.4 ANALYZING THE MODELS

The different multi-tenancy models provide different trade-offs; Figure 6.1 depicts some of these trade-offs as we move from the shared hardware model to the shared table model. At one extreme, the *shared hardware* model uses virtualization to multiplex multiple VMs on the same machine. Each VM has only a single database process serving the database of a single tenant. As mentioned earlier, this strong tenant isolation comes at the cost of reduced performance [Curino et al., 2011b]. At the other extreme is the *shared table* model that stores multiple tenants' data in shared tables and provides the least amount of isolation, which in turn requires changes to the database engine while limiting schema flexibility across the tenants. The *shared process* model allows independent schemas

---

[2]This support is facilitated in commercial DBMS engines to enable hosting of different types of databases: production DB, quality assurance DB, development DB, etc.

Table 6.1: Multi-tenant database models, how tenants are isolated, and the corresponding cloud computing paradigms.

#	Sharing Mode	Isolation	IaaS	PaaS	SaaS
1.	*Shared hardware*	VM	✓		
2.	*Shared VM*	OS User	✓	✓	
3.	*Shared OS*	DB Instance		✓	
4.	*Shared instance*	Database		✓	
5.	*Shared database*	Schema		✓	✓
6.	*Shared table*	Row		✓	✓

for tenants while sharing the database process among multiple tenants, thus providing better isolation compared to the shared table model while allowing effective sharing and consolidation of multiple tenants in the same database process. The shared process model therefore strikes the middle ground.

While broad in concept, three main paradigms have emerged for cloud computing: IaaS, PaaS, and SaaS. These cloud computing paradigms differ in the level of abstraction exposed to the tenants. For instance, IaaS exposes raw hardware resources to the tenants and the tenants are responsible for managing their own DBMSs, schemas, physical database design, backup, etc. IaaS therefore provides the lowest level of abstraction. PaaS provides a higher level of abstraction where the tenants interact with logical databases and resources and often do not control the physical data layout, replication, etc. SaaS exposes the highest level of abstraction where the tenants interact at the level of application logic with no (or minimal) knowledge of the data layout, schemas, physical structures, query workloads, etc.

We now establish the connection between the database multi-tenancy models with the cloud computing paradigms. While the three multi-tenancy models discussed above are well known, Reinwald [2010] presented a finer classification where each model was further sub-divided depending on the exact level of sharing. Table 6.1 summarizes this taxonomy while analyzing the suitability of the models for various multi-tenancy scenarios. Finer sub-divisions of the shared hardware model (where the tenants still do not share the database process) are *shared VM*, where the tenants share a VM and are isolated as different OS-level user logins, and the *shared OS* model, where tenants share the same OS but each have their own dedicated database process. Finer sub-divisions of the shared process model (where tenants share the database process but do not share the physical tables) are *shared instance* and *shared database*.

IaaS provides raw resources such as CPU, storage, and networking. Supporting multi-tenancy in the IaaS layer thus allows much flexibility with minimal restrictions on tenant schemas or workload supported. The *shared hardware* model is therefore best suited for IaaS. A simple multi-tenant system could be built on a cluster of commodity machines, each with a small set of virtual machines. This model provides isolation, security, and efficient migration for the client databases with an acceptable overhead, and is suitable for applications with lower throughput but larger storage requirements.

PaaS providers, on the other hand, provide a higher level of abstraction to the tenants. There exists a wide class of PaaS providers, and a single multi-tenant database model cannot be a blanket choice. For PaaS systems that provide a single data store API, a *shared table* or *shared instance* could meet data needs of this platform. For instance, Google App Engine uses the shared table model for its data store referred to as Megastore. However, PaaS systems with the flexibility to support a variety of data stores, such as AppScale [Chohan et al., 2009], can leverage any multi-tenant database model.

SaaS has the highest level of abstraction in which a client uses the service to perform a limited and focused task. Customization is typically superficial, and workflows or data models are primarily dictated by the service provider. With rigid definitions for both data and processes, and restricted access to a data layer through a web service or browser, the service provider has control over how the tenants interact with the data store. The *shared table* model has thus been successfully used by various SaaS providers.

6.2   DATABASE ELASTICITY IN THE CLOUD

One of the major factors for the success of the cloud as an IT infrastructure is its *pay per use* pricing model and *elasticity*. For a DBMS deployed on a pay-per-use cloud infrastructure, an added goal is to optimize the system's operating cost. *Elasticity*, i.e., the ability to deal with load variations by adding more resources during high load or consolidating the tenants to fewer nodes when the load decreases, all in a live system without service disruption, is therefore critical for these systems.

The overall vision of multi-tenancy in cloud computing platforms is to develop an architecture of a multi-tenant DBMS that is *scalable, fault-tolerant, elastic,* and *self-managing.* We envision multi-tenancy as analogous to virtualization in the database tier for sharing the DBMS resources. Similar to virtual machine migration [Clark et al., 2005], efficient techniques for live database migration is an integral component for elastic load balancing. Live database migration should therefore be a first-class feature in the system having the same stature as scalability, consistency, and fault-tolerance. Only recently, there have been an increase in research and development efforts in the areas of live database migration for elastic load balancing.

Even though elasticity is often associated with the scale of the system, a subtle difference exists between elasticity and scalability when used to express a system's behavior. Scalability is a static property of the system that specifies its behavior on a static configuration. For instance, a system design might scale to hundreds or even to thousands of nodes. On the other hand, elasticity is a dynamic property that allows the system's scale to be increased or decreased *on-demand* while the system is operational. For instance, a system design is elastic if it can scale from 10 servers to 20 servers (or vice-versa) on-demand.

Elasticity is a desirable and important property of large-scale systems. For a system deployed on a pay-per-use cloud service, such as the Infrastructure as a Service (IaaS) abstraction, elasticity is critical to minimize operating cost while ensuring good performance during high loads. It allows consolidation of the system to consume less resources and thus minimize the operating cost during periods of low load while allowing it to dynamically scale up its size as the load decreases. On the other hand, enterprise infrastructures are often statically provisioned. Elasticity is also desirable in scenarios where energy efficiency is critical. Even though the infrastructure is statically provisioned, significant savings can be achieved by consolidating tenants and therefore powering down servers, thus reducing the power usage and cooling costs. This, however, is an open research topic in its own merit, since powering down random servers does not necessarily reduce energy usage. Careful planning is needed to select servers to power down such that entire racks and alleys in a data-center are powered down so that significant savings in cooling can be achieved. One must also consider the impact of powering down on availability. For instance, consolidating the system to a set of servers all within a single point of failure (for instance a switch or a power supply unit) can result in an entire service outage resulting from a single failure. Furthermore, bringing up powered down servers is more expensive, so the penalty for a mispredicted power down operation is higher.

In our context of a database system, migrating parts of a system while the system is operational is important to achieve on-demand elasticity. This can be achieved via an operation called *live database migration*. While being elastic, the system must also ensure that a tenant's performance or service goals are not violated. Therefore, to be effectively used for elasticity, live migration must have low impact, i.e., negligible effect on performance and minimal service interruption on the tenant being migrated as well as other tenants co-located at the source and destination of migration.

Since migration is a necessary primitive for achieving elasticity, we focus on describing recent proposals for live migration for the two most common cloud database architectures: shared disk and shared nothing. Shared disk architectures are attractive for their ability to abstract replication, fault-tolerance, and consistency, as well as their support for independent scaling of the storage layer from the DBMS logic. Bigtable, HBase, and ElasTraS are examples of databases that use a shared disk architecture. On the other hand, a shared nothing multi-tenant architecture, such as Relational Cloud and Cloud SQL Server, uses locally attached storage for storing the persistent data and are common in database design. Live migration for a shared nothing architecture requires that all database components are migrated between nodes, including physical storage files. Since this chapter discusses multi-tenant systems, in this section, we use the term tenant to refer to the database granule being migrated. However, most of the live migration techniques presented here can be used to migrate any self-contained granule of the database, such as a partition of a large-scale database (as discussed in previous chapters).

6.2.1   ALBATROSS: LIVE MIGRATION FOR SHARED STORAGE DATA STORES

The underlying reference system model used in Albatross is depicted in Figure 6.2. This model assumes the shared process multi-tenancy model where a tenant is entirely contained in a single database process; multiple tenants are co-located within a single database process. Application clients connect through a *decentralized query router* which abstracts physical database connections as logical connections between a tenant and the database server processing the tenant's requests. The mapping of a tenant to its server is stored as *system metadata* which is cached by the router.

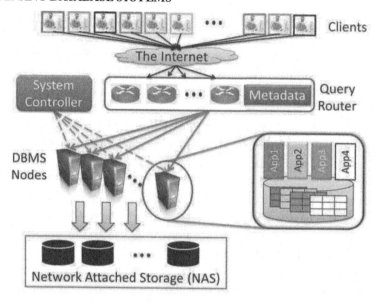

Figure 6.2: Reference database system model.

A cluster of *DBMS nodes* serves the tenants; each node has its own local transaction manager (*TM*) and data manager (*DM*). A TM consists of a *concurrency control* component for transaction execution and a *recovery component* to deal with failures. A tenant is served by a single DBMS node, called its *owner*. The size of a tenant is therefore limited by the capacity of a single DBMS node. This unique ownership allows transactions to execute efficiently without distributed synchronization among multiple DBMS nodes.

A network attached storage (*NAS*) provides a scalable, highly available, and fault-tolerant storage of the persistent data of the tenant databases. This *decoupling* of storage from ownership obviates the need to copy a tenant's persistent data during migration. This architecture is however different from shared disk systems that use the disk for arbitration among concurrent transaction [Bernstein and Newcomer, 2009]. A system *controller* performs control operations including determining the tenant to migrate, the destination, and the time to initiate migration.

Albatross aims to have minimal impact on tenant performance while leveraging the semantics of the database structures for efficient database migration. This is achieved by iteratively transferring the database cache and the state of active transactions. For a 2PL scheduler, the transaction state consists of the lock table; for an OCC scheduler, this state consists of the read-write sets of active transactions and a subset of committed transactions. Figure 6.3 depicts the timeline of Albatross when migrating a tenant (P_{migr}) from the source DBMS node (N_{src}) to the destination DBMS node (N_{dst}). The overall migration process proceeds in multiple phases which are detailed below.

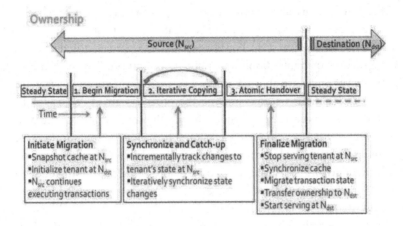

Figure 6.3: Migration timeline for Albatross (times not drawn to scale).

Phase 1: *Begin Migration:* Migration is initiated by creating a snapshot of the database cache at N_{src}. This snapshot is then copied to N_{dst}. N_{src} continues processing transactions while this copying is in progress.

Phase 2: *Iterative Copying:* Since N_{src} continues serving transactions for P_{migr} while N_{dst} is initialized with the snapshot, the cached state of P_{migr} at N_{dst} will lag that of N_{src}. In this iterative phase, at every iteration, N_{dst} tries to "catch up" and synchronize the state of P_{migr} at N_{src} and N_{dst}. N_{src} tracks changes made to the database cache between two consecutive iterations. In iteration i, changes made to P_{migr}'s cache since the snapshot of iteration $i - 1$ are copied to N_{dst}. This phase is terminated when approximately the same amount of state is transferred in consecutive iterations or a configurable maximum number of iterations have completed.

Phase 3: *Atomic Handover:* In this phase, the exclusive read/write access of P_{migr} (called *ownership*) is transferred from N_{src} to N_{dst}. N_{src} stops serving P_{migr}, copies the final unsynchronized database state and the state of active transactions to N_{dst}, flushes changes from *committed* transactions to the persistent storage, transfers control of P_{migr} to N_{dst}, and notifies the *query router* of the new location of P_{migr}. To ensure safety in the presence of failures, this operation is guaranteed to be *atomic*. The successful completion of this phase makes N_{dst} the owner of P_{migr} and completes the migration.

The iterative phase minimizes the amount of P_{migr}'s state to be copied and flushed in the handover phase, thus minimizing the unavailability window. In the case where the transaction logic is executed at the client, transactions are seamlessly transferred from N_{src} to N_{dst} without any loss of work. The handover phase copies the state of active transaction along with the database cache. For a 2PL scheduler, it copies the lock table state and reassigns the appropriate locks and latches at N_{dst}; for an OCC scheduler, it copies the read/write sets of the active transactions and that of a subset of committed transactions whose state is needed to validate new transactions. For a 2PL scheduler, updates of active transactions are done in place in the database cache and hence are copied over during the final copy phase; in OCC, the local writes of the active transactions are copied to N_{dst} along with the transaction state. For transactions executed as stored procedures, N_{src} tracks the invocation parameters of transactions active during migration. Any such transactions active at the start of the handover phase are aborted at N_{src}, and are automatically restarted at N_{dst}. This allows migrating these transactions without moving the process state at N_{src}. Durability of transactions that committed at N_{src} is ensured by synchronizing the commit logs of the two nodes.

In the event of a failure, data safety is paramount while progress toward successful completion of migration is a secondary goal. Albatross's failure model assumes reliable communication channels, node failures, and network partitions, but no malicious node behavior. Node failures do not lead to complete loss of data: either the node recovers or the data are recovered from the NAS where data persist beyond DBMS node failures. If either N_{src} or N_{dst} fails prior to Phase 3, migration of P_{migr} is aborted. Progress made in migration is not logged until Phase 3. If N_{src} fails during Phases 1 or 2, its state is recovered, but since there is no persistent information of migration in the commit log of N_{src}, the progress made in P_{migr}'s migration is lost during this recovery. N_{dst} eventually detects this failure and in turn aborts this migration. If N_{dst} fails, migration is again aborted since N_{dst} does not have any log entries for a migration in progress. Thus, in case of failure of either node, migration is aborted and the recovery of a node does not require coordination with any other node in the system.

The atomic handover phase (Phase 3) consists of the following major steps: (*i*) flushing changes from all committed transactions at N_{src}; (*ii*) synchronizing the remaining state of P_{migr} between N_{src} and N_{dst}; (*iii*) transferring ownership of P_{migr} from N_{src} to N_{dst}; and (*iv*) notifying the query router that all future transactions must be routed to N_{dst}. Steps (iii) and (iv) can only be performed after the completion of Steps (i) and (ii). Ownership transfer involves three participants—N_{src}, N_{dst}, and the query router—and must be atomic (i.e., either all or nothing). This handover is executed as an *atomic transfer transaction* and a 2PC protocol, with N_{src} as the coordinator, guarantees atomicity in the presence of failures. In the first phase, N_{src} executes steps (i) and (ii) in parallel, and solicits a vote from the participants. Once all the nodes acknowledge the operations and vote *yes*, the transfer transaction enters the second phase where N_{src} relinquishes control of P_{migr} and transfers it to N_{dst}. In the case when one of the participants votes *no*, this *transfer transaction* is aborted and N_{src} remains the owner of P_{migr}. This second step completes the transfer transaction at N_{src} which, after logging the outcome, notifies the participants about the decision. If the handover was successful, N_{dst} assumes ownership of P_{migr} once it receives the notification from N_{src}. Every protocol action is logged in the commit log of the respective nodes. Formal reasoning for the correctness guarantees and detailed evaluation of Albatross appear in [Das, 2011].

6.2.2   ZEPHYR: LIVE MIGRATION FOR SHARED NOTHING DATA STORES

Zephyr assumes a standard shared-nothing database model for transaction processing (OLTP) systems executing short running transactions, with a 2PL scheduler, and a page-based model with a B+ tree index. Figure 6.4 provides an overview of the architecture. Following are the salient features

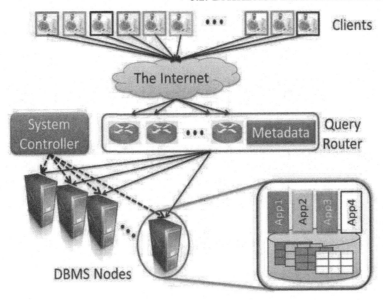

Figure 6.4: A shared nothing multi-tenant DBMS architecture.

of the system. First, clients connect to the database through *query routers* that handle client connections and hide the physical location of the tenant's database. Routers store this mapping as metadata which is updated whenever there is a migration. Second, Zephyr assumes the *shared process* multi-tenancy model that strikes a balance between isolation and scale. Conceptually, each tenant has its own transaction manager and buffer pool. However, since most current systems do not support this, Zephyr assumes a design where co-located tenants share all resources within a database instance, but is shared nothing across nodes. Finally, there exists a *system controller* that determines the tenant to be migrated, the initiation time, and the destination of migration. The system controller gathers usage statistics and builds a model to optimize the system's operating cost while guaranteeing the tenant's performance goals. The detailed design and implementation of the controller is orthogonal and is reviewed under the issue of *autonomic control* of multi-tenant databases in the cloud (see Section 6.3). Zephyr also makes some simplifying assumptions about the underlying system model: it assumes small tenant footprints limited to a single node in the system, and no replication; furthermore, the index structures are made immutable during migration, i.e., if a transaction update will result in a structural change to the underlying index structure then the offending transaction is aborted.

Zephyr's main design goal is to minimize the service interruption resulting from migrating a tenant's database ($\mathbb{D}_M$). Zephyr does not incur a stop phase where $\mathbb{D}_M$ is unavailable for executing updates; it uses a sequence of three modes to allow the migration of $\mathbb{D}_M$ while transactions are executing on it. During normal operation (called the *normal mode*), $\mathbb{N}_S$ is the node serving $\mathbb{D}_M$ and executing all transactions $T_{S1}, \ldots, T_{Sk}$ on $\mathbb{D}_M$. A node that has the rights to execute update

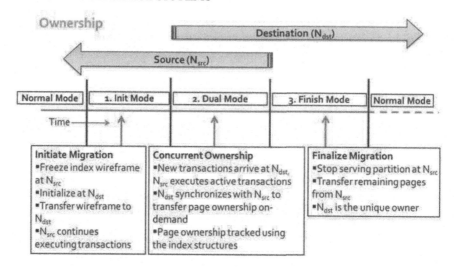

Figure 6.5: Timeline for different phases of Zephyr.

transactions on $\mathbb{D}_M$ is called the *owner* of $\mathbb{D}_M$. Once the system controller determines the destination for migration ($\mathbb{N}_D$), it notifies $\mathbb{N}_S$ which initiates migration to $\mathbb{N}_D$. Figure 6.5 shows the timeline of this migration algorithm and the control and data messages exchanged between the nodes. As time progresses from the left to right, Figure 6.5 shows the progress of the different migration modes, starting from the *init mode* that initiates migration, the *dual mode* where both $\mathbb{N}_S$ and $\mathbb{N}_D$ share the ownership of $\mathbb{D}_M$ and simultaneously execute transactions on $\mathbb{D}_M$, and the *Finish Mode* which is the last step of migration before $\mathbb{N}_D$ assumes full ownership of $\mathbb{D}_M$. Figure 6.6 shows the transition of $\mathbb{D}_M$'s data through the three migration modes, depicted using ownership of database pages and executing transactions.

Init Mode: In the init mode, $\mathbb{N}_S$ bootstraps $\mathbb{N}_D$ by sending the minimal information (the *wireframe* of $\mathbb{D}_M$) such that $\mathbb{N}_D$ can execute transactions on $\mathbb{D}_M$. The wireframe consists of the schema and data definitions of $\mathbb{D}_M$, index structures, and user authentication information. Indices migrated include the internal nodes of the clustered index storing the database and all secondary indices. Non-indexed attributes are accessed through the clustered index. In this mode, $\mathbb{N}_S$ is still the unique owner of $\mathbb{D}_M$ and executes transactions $(T_{S1}, \ldots, T_{Sk})$ without synchronizing with any other node. Therefore, there is no service interruption for $\mathbb{D}_M$ while $\mathbb{N}_D$ initializes the necessary resources for $\mathbb{D}_M$. We assume a B+ tree index, where the internal nodes of the index contain only the keys while the actual data pages are in the leaves. The wireframe, therefore, only includes these internal nodes of the indices for the database tables. Figure 6.7 illustrates this, where the part of the tree enclosed in a rectangular box is the *index wireframe*. At $\mathbb{N}_S$, the wireframe is constructed with minimal impact on concurrent operations using shared multi-granularity intention locks on the indices. When $\mathbb{N}_D$ receives the wireframe, it has $\mathbb{D}_M$'s metadata, but the data are still owned by $\mathbb{N}_S$. Since migration

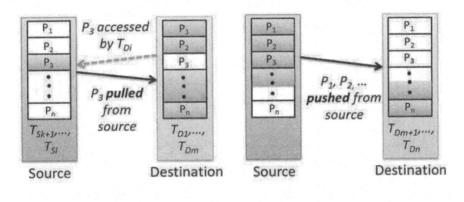

(a) Dual Mode.

(b) Finish Mode.

Figure 6.6: Ownership transfer of the database pages during migration. P_i represents a database page and a white box around P_i represents that the node currently *owns* the page.

involves a gradual transfer of page-level ownership, both N_S and N_D must maintain a list of owned pages. We use the B+ tree index for tracking page ownership. A valid pointer to a database page implies unique page ownership, while a sentinel value (NULL) indicates a missing page. In the init mode, N_D therefore initializes all the pointers to the leaf nodes of the index to the sentinel value. Once N_D completes initialization of $\mathbb{D}_M$, it notifies N_S, which then initiates the transition to the dual mode. N_S then executes the *atomic handover* protocol which notifies the *query router* to direct all new transactions to N_D.

Dual Mode: In the dual mode, both N_S and N_D execute transactions on $\mathbb{D}_M$, and database pages are migrated to N_D *on-demand*. All new transactions $(T_{D1}, \ldots, T_{Dm})$ arrive at N_D, while N_S continues executing transactions that were active at the start of this mode $(T_{Sk+1}, \ldots, T_{Sl})$. Since N_S and N_D share ownership of $\mathbb{D}_M$, they synchronize to ensure transaction correctness. Zephyr, however, requires minimal synchronization between these nodes.

At N_S, transactions execute normally using local index and page-level locking, until a transaction T_{Sj} accesses a page P_j which has already been migrated. In the current design of Zephyr, a database page is migrated only once. Therefore, such an access fails and the transaction is aborted. When a transaction T_{Di} executing at N_D accesses a page P_i that is not owned by N_D, it *pulls* P_i from N_S *on demand* (pull phase as shown in Figure 6.6(a)); this pull request is serviced only if P_i is not locked at N_S, in which case the request is blocked. As the pages are migrated, both N_S and N_D update their ownership mapping. Once N_D receives P_i, it proceeds to execute T_{Di}. Apart from fetching missing pages from N_S, transactions at N_S and N_D do not need to synchronize. Due to the critical assumption in Zephyr that the index structure cannot change at N_S once migration is initiated, local

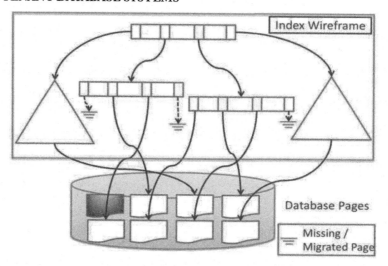

Figure 6.7: B+ tree index structure with page ownership information. A sentinel marks missing pages. An allocated database page without ownership is represented as a grayed page.

locking of the index structure and pages is enough. This ensures minimal synchronization between $\mathbb{N}_S$ and $\mathbb{N}_D$ only during this short dual mode, while ensuring serializable transaction execution.

When $\mathbb{N}_S$ has finished executing all transactions $T_{Sk+1}, \ldots, T_{Sl}$ that were active at the start of dual mode (i.e. $\mathbb{T}(\mathbb{N}_S) = \phi$), it initiates transfer of exclusive ownership to $\mathbb{N}_D$. This transfer is achieved through a handshake between $\mathbb{N}_S$ and $\mathbb{N}_D$ after which both nodes enter the finish mode for $\mathbb{D}_M$.

Finish Mode: In the finish mode, $\mathbb{N}_D$ is the only node executing transactions on $\mathbb{D}_M$ ($T_{Dm+1}, \ldots, T_{Dn}$), but does not yet have ownership of all the database pages (Figure 6.6(b)). In this phase, $\mathbb{N}_S$ *pushes* the remaining database pages to $\mathbb{N}_D$. While the pages are migrated from $\mathbb{N}_S$, if a transaction T_{Di} accesses a page that is not yet owned by $\mathbb{N}_D$, the page is requested as a *pull* from $\mathbb{N}_S$ in a way similar to that in the dual mode. Ideally, $\mathbb{N}_S$ must migrate the pages at the highest possible transfer rate such that the delays resulting from $\mathbb{N}_D$ fetching missing pages is minimized. However, such a high throughput push can impact other tenants co-located at $\mathbb{N}_S$ and $\mathbb{N}_D$. Therefore, the rate of transfer is a trade-off between the performance impact on the tenant and the migration overhead. The page ownership information is also updated during this bulk transfer. When all the database pages have been moved to $\mathbb{N}_D$, $\mathbb{N}_S$ initiates the termination of migration so that operation switches back to the normal mode. This again involves a handshake between $\mathbb{N}_S$ and $\mathbb{N}_D$. On successful completion of this handshake, it is guaranteed that $\mathbb{N}_D$ has a persistent image of $\mathbb{D}_M$, and so $\mathbb{N}_S$ can safely release all of $\mathbb{D}_M$'s resources. $\mathbb{N}_D$ executes transactions on $\mathbb{D}_M$ without any interaction with $\mathbb{N}_S$. Once migration terminates, $\mathbb{N}_S$ notifies the system controller.

The correctness of transactions execution during migration in Zephyr can be established assuming that a concurrency protocol such as 2PL is used by the underlying architecture. In the init mode and finish mode, only one of N_S and N_D is executing transactions on $\mathbb{D}_M$. The init mode is equivalent to normal operation while in finish mode, N_S acts as the storage node for the database serving pages on demand. Guaranteeing serializability is straightforward in these two modes. Reasoning about correctness in the dual mode is more involved since both N_S and N_D are executing transactions on $\mathbb{D}_M$. In the dual mode, N_S and N_D share the internal nodes of the index which are immutable due to Zephyr's underlying assumption, while the leaf nodes (i.e. the data pages) are still uniquely owned by at most one of the two nodes. Note that if a cycle in a serialization graph arises during dual mode, then it must be the case that there is an edge in the conflict graph of the form $T_{Di} \rightarrow T_{Sj}$. But existence of such an edge will violate the property of Zephyr that migrates data pages only once and only in one direction from N_S to N_D. A complete proof of correctness appears in [Elmore et al., 2011].

Zephyr's failure model assumes that all message transfers use reliable communication channels that guarantee in-order, at most once delivery. Zephyr assumes node crash failures and network partitions; but assumes that there is no malicious node behavior. Furthermore, it is assumed that a node failure does not lead to loss of the persistent disk image. In case of a failure during migration, Zephyr first recovers the state of the committed transactions and then recovers the state of migration.

Transaction State Recovery. Transactions executing during migration use write ahead logging for transaction state recovery. Hence, after a crash, a node recovers its transaction state using standard log replay techniques such as ARIES [Mohan et al., 1992]. In the dual mode, N_S and N_D append transactions to their respective node's local transaction log. Log entries in a single log file have a local order. However, since the log for $\mathbb{D}_M$ is spread over N_S and N_D, a logical global order of transactions on $\mathbb{D}_M$ is needed to ensure that the transactions from the two logs are applied in the correct order to recover from a failure during migration. The ordering of transactions is important only when there is a conflict between two transactions. If two transactions, T_S and T_D, executing on N_S and N_D, conflict on item i, they must access the same database page P_i. Since at any instant of time only one of N_S and N_D is the owner of P_i, the two nodes must synchronize to arbitrate on P_i. This synchronization forms the basis for establishing a total order between the transactions. During migration, a *commit sequence number* (CSN) is assigned to every transaction at commit time, and is appended along with the commit record of the transaction. This CSN is a monotonically increasing sequence number maintained locally at the nodes and determines the order in which transactions commit. If P_i was owned by N_S and T_S was the last committed transaction before the migration request for P_i was made, then $CSN(T_S)$ is piggy-backed with P_i. On receipt of a page P_i, N_D sets its CSN as the maximum of its local CSN and that received with P_i such that at N_D, $CSN(T_D) > CSN(T_S)$. This causal conflict ordering creates a global order per database page, where all transactions at N_S accessing P_i are ordered before all transactions at N_D that access P_i.

Migration State Recovery. Migration progress is logged to guarantee atomicity and consistency in the presence of failures. A failure of either N_S or N_D in the dual mode or the finish mode requires coordinated recovery between the two nodes. During migration, a transition from one state to another is logged. Except for the transition from the init mode to dual mode, which involves the query router metadata in addition to N_S and N_D, all other transitions involve only N_S and N_D. Such transitions occur through a one-phase handshake between N_S and N_D (as shown in Figure 6.5). At the occurrence of an event triggering a state transition, N_S initiates the transition by sending a message to N_D. On receipt of the message, N_D moves to the next migration mode, forces a log entry for this change, and sends an acknowledgment to N_S. Receipt of this acknowledgment completes this transition and N_S forces another entry to its log. If N_S fails before sending the message to N_D, the mode remains unchanged when N_S recovers, and N_S re-initiates the transition. If N_S fails after sending the message, then it knows about the message after it recovers and establishes contact with N_D. The transition from the init mode to the dual mode involves three participants (N_S, N_D, and the query router metadata) that must together change the state and hence the 2PC protocol is used and atomicity of this handover process in a distributed environment follows directly from the atomicity property of 2PC. The page ownership information is critical for migration progress as well as safety. A simple fault-tolerant design is to make this ownership information durable—any page (P_i) transferred from N_S is immediately flushed to the disk at N_D. N_S also makes this transfer persistent, either by logging the transfer or by updating P_i's parent page in the index, and flushing it to the disk. This simple solution will guarantee resilience to failure but introduces a lot of disk I/O which considerably increases migration cost and impacts other co-located tenants. Elmore et al. [2011] discuss several optimizations for such scenarios.

6.2.3   SLACKER: LIVE DBMS INSTANCE MIGRATION IN SHARED-NOTHING MODEL

We now briefly summarize the design of Slacker [Barker et al., 2012] that is in contrast to the two approaches presented above for live database migration. Slacker is a system that performs rapid database migrations while minimizing the costs of migration, namely, system downtime, tenant interference, and human intervention. Slacker is a component of NEC's comprehensive data management platform for the cloud, CloudDB [Hacigümüs et al., 2010, Tatemura et al., 2012]. The underlying design philosophy of Slacker can be summarized as follows:

- Slacker is intended as a technique for performing live (zero-downtime) database migration using standard database backup tools. Unlike other live database migration techniques, Slacker is unique in that it operates on off-the-shelf database systems using readily available open-source tools. It does not require modifications to the database engine and can be implemented completely outside of a database product.

- Slacker uses the idea of *migration slack*, which refers to resources that can be used for migration without seriously impacting workloads already present on the database server. A formal mathematical model to continuously monitor this slack is used in the implementation to minimize interference through the use of migration throttling. This approach is based on a novel application of control theory.

Slacker is implemented as a middleware that sits atop one or more MySQL tenants. Each server running an instance of Slacker operates a single server-wide migration controller that migrates MySQL instances on the server to other servers running Slacker. In addition to migrating existing tenants, the middleware is also responsible for instantiating (or deleting) MySQL instances for new tenants. Each Slacker node operates in an autonomous fashion and only communicates with other nodes for the purpose of migrating tenants.

Slacker interacts with MySQL backend databases using InnoDB tables.[3] The multi-tenancy model in Slacker is process-level—that is, each tenant co-located on the server is provided a dedicated MySQL daemon listening on a dedicated port. Each tenant has full control over its daemon and is free to create arbitrary databases, tables, and users. Adding a tenant creates a new data directory containing all MySQL data, including table data, logs, and configuration files. Similarly, deleting a tenant simply stops the server process and deletes the tenant's data directory. From Slacker's perspective, each tenant is simply a directory containing all data and a corresponding MySQL process. Slacker is transparent to tenants, who need not be aware of Slacker at all and simply interact directly with their MySQL server on the assigned port.

The choice of process-level multi-tenancy rather than a single, consolidated database server (housing all tenants) has two primary advantages. The first is increased isolation between tenants, since each database server treats its tenant on a best-effort basis. This prevents situations such as buffer page evictions due to competing workloads—thus avoiding any situations in which buffer allocations overlap by never over-provisioning memory. The second is ease of engineering, since resources belonging to each tenant are cleanly separated on the server. These advantages come at the cost of modest per-tenant memory overhead and decreased maximum throughput relative to a consolidated DBMS [Curino et al., 2011a].

Slacker itself is implemented as a Java framework to create, delete, and migrate database tenants. The migration controller on each server monitors all tenants located on the machine and manages any in-progress migrations. Tenants are represented by globally unique numeric IDs, which are used to issue commands to Slacker (such as *Migrate Tenant 5 to Server x*). Communication between Slacker migration controllers occurs in a peer-to-peer fashion using a simple format based on Google's protocol buffers [Google Protocol Buffers]. Migrations are performed on-demand by connecting to another control node and initiating the migration of a specific tenant. For customer applications, communication with a specific tenant database requires only knowledge of the machine on which the tenant is located and the tenant ID, since the database port is a fixed function of the ID. This approach is only problematic after a migration is performed, since the tenant no longer

---

[3]InnoDB is a high-reliability, high-performance, and ACID-compliant storage engine for MySQL. http://dev.mysql.com/doc/refman/5.0/en/innodb-storage-engine.html.

resides on the original server. This issue can be resolved cleanly by issuing an ARP packet advertising a new IP address (similar to [Clark et al., 2005]).

Live migration in Slacker uses the tool Percona XtraBackup [Percona], which is an extended, open-source version of the commercial MySQL Enterprise Backup program. Mainly intended for the purpose of hot backup, XtraBackup produces a consistent-in-time snapshot of the database without interrupting transaction processing. Slacker leverages this hot backup function to obtain a consistent snapshot for use in starting a new MySQL instance. Migration in Slacker is performed in three steps. In the initial snapshot transferring step, Slacker streams the initial snapshot generated by XtraBackup to the destination server on-the-fly, then prepares the snapshot on the destination while the source continues to service queries. During preparation, XtraBackup applies crash recovery against the copied data. Due to the time spent preparing the snapshot, once the destination server is running, it may be somewhat behind the still authoritative source server. To allow the destination to catch up with the source, Slacker iteratively applies incremental updates from the source to the destination, an approach similar to the iterative phase of Albatross. In this step, called the Δ updating step, Slacker applies several *rounds* of δ_is from the source to the destination by reading from the MySQL binary query log of the source. Each δ_i comprises the changes from the update transactions processed at the source since the snapshot from the previous iteration. Each such δ_i brings the destination up-to-date at the point where the δ_i began executing. The subsequent δ_{i+1} contains changes corresponding to transactions that executed when δ_i was being applied to the destination. Once δ_is are sufficiently small, in the handover step, a very brief freeze-and-handover is performed during which the source is frozen, the final δ_N is copied, and the target becomes the new authoritative tenant. A more detailed analysis and evaluation of Slacker appears in [Barker et al., 2012].

6.3   AUTONOMIC CONTROL FOR DATABASE WORKLOADS IN THE CLOUD

Managing large systems poses significant challenges in monitoring, management, and system operation. Moreover, to reduce the operating cost, considerable autonomy is needed in the administration of such systems. In the context of database systems, the responsibilities of this autonomic controller include monitoring the behavior and performance of the system, elastic scaling, and load balancing based on dynamic usage patterns, modeling behavior to forecast workload spikes and take proactive measures to handle such spikes. An autonomous and intelligent system controller is essential to properly manage such large systems.

Modeling the behavior of a database system and performance tuning has been an active area of research over the last couple of decades. A large body of work focuses on tuning the appropriate parameters for optimizing database performance [Duan et al., 2009, Weikum et al., 2002], primarily in the context of a single database server. Another line of work has focused on resource prediction, provisioning, and placement in large distributed systems [Bodík et al., 2008, Urgaonkar et al., 2007].

Live VM Migration and tools such as VMWare's Distributed Resource Scheduler [DRS] are used for automated placement of virtual machines on a cluster of hosts for effective and efficient

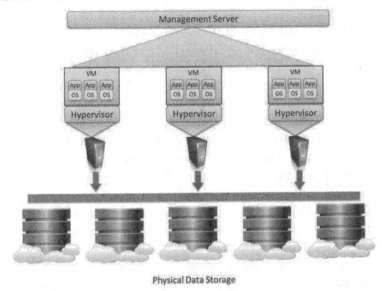

Figure 6.8: Storage virtualization architecture in large data centers.

management of CPU and memory resources. More recently, companies such as VMware are realizing the need for automatic placement and load balancing of I/O workloads across a set of storage devices especially since diverse I/O behavior from various workloads and hot-spotting can cause significant imbalance. Thus, the need for autonomic control exists for virtualized storage management in data-centers (see Figure 6.8) and given its close relationship with database multi-tenancy, we review recent results in this area. Note that our discussion here is representative and is not meant to be comprehensive. An extensive body of work exists both in the area of autonomic computing, in general, and virtualized storage management, in particular.

The need for automated storage management arises in virtualized environments due to a high degree of storage consolidation and sprawl of virtual disks over tens to hundreds of data stores. Figure 6.8 illustrates a typical configuration of computing and storage resources in a data center. Initial placement of virtual disks and data migration across different physical data stores needs to be based on workload characterization, device model, and analytic formulation to improve I/O performance and utilization. VMware has developed BASIL [Gulati et al., 2010], which is a tool designed to automate I/O load balancing across multiple storage devices. The key features of BASIL are that it postulates I/O latency as being the key metric for overall system performance and it provides simple models for online characterization of workloads and device behaviors. In particular, through extensive empirical observations BASIL demonstrates that I/O latency has a linear relationship with the number of outstanding I/O requests on a device. BASIL hence uses the latency as a key metric to control the placement and migration of virtual disks and data across physical storage devices.

BASIL has been in use in production, and VMware has recently reported several challenges associated with its use in real deployment scenarios. One of the problems is that the BASIL model is based on passive observations of actual workloads, causing different models to be produced for the same device over time. The other problem is that robust model creation in BASIL requires covering a wide range of outstanding I/O requests, which may not be observed in production deployments, even over long time periods. Furthermore, BASIL does not perform cost-benefit analysis (i.e., the cost of data migration versus the potential improvements in throughput or latency) during autonomic control. As a result, the development group at VMware have proposed a new system called Pesto [Gulati et al., 2011] that overcomes these limitations. The underlying modeling principles of Pesto is still based on the linear relationship between latency and outstanding I/O requests on a device.

Autonomic control of database-driven applications in the data center has emerged as an important problem since a single data center within an organization may deploy hundreds or even thousands of individual DBMSs. Database multi-tenancy where multiple databases can be consolidated by analyzing the workload characteristics of multiple dedicated database servers and packing their workloads into fewer physical machines is of significant value. As discussed above, consolidating servers is not a new idea and has been the driver for widespread deployment of virtual machines and virtual storage in data centers. However, consolidating databases is harder since DBMSs make strong assumptions regarding the characteristics and performance of the underlying physical system.

Curino et al. [2011b] have developed a system called Kairos for workload-aware database monitoring and consolidation. Kairos tackles two major challenges: (i) it develops tools to accurately monitor the resource utilization of each database and to estimate the utilization of a combined set of databases consolidated within a single instance of a DBMS; and (ii) it provides algorithms for the placement of databases on physical hardware. Kairos begins with a set of independent database workloads running on dedicated servers. The output from Kairos is a consolidation strategy mapping workloads to physical nodes. After consolidation, each physical node runs a *single* DBMS instance hosting multiple databases while meeting the applications' service-level requirements. In that sense Kairos supports the *shared process* model of multitenancy.

Kairos architecture comprises three major components: (i) Resource Monitor; (ii) Combined Load Estimator; and (iii) Consolidation Engine. The *resource monitor* collects performance statistics from the DBMS engine and the operating system to estimate the resource consumption and characterize the workload of individual databases in an online manner. The *combined load estimator* uses the workload characterization of individual databases running on dedicated hardware as an input and runs an algorithm to predict the performance characteristics of combined workloads in a single database. Modeling the interaction is especially challenging for disk I/O, since disk throughput is a complicated nonlinear function of the load, which is in contrast to the CPU or memory which in general combine linearly. Kairos overcomes this challenge by developing a hardware-specific model for a given DBMS allowing it to evaluate the performance of arbitrary combinations of the different types of workloads. Finally, the *consolidation engine* in Kairos uses nonlinear optimization techniques to find assignments of databases onto physical resources subject to the following constraints: (i) the number of machines are minimized; (ii) load balance across the machine is maximized; and (iii) and service-level requirements of each workload will be met.

Note that even though Kairos is a significant advance toward autonomic control in multi-tenant database environments, but it is still a first step. In particular, Kairos solves the initial step toward multi-tenancy by generating an optimal assignment of tenant databases on physical machines in the *shared process* multitenancy model. This placement will work as long as the workload characteristics of individual tenants remain the same. However, in reality, tenant workloads vary over time and therefore there is a need for continuous monitoring of consolidated tenant placement and there is a need to develop an online algorithm that re-adjusts tenant occupancies to respond to workload variations. Furthermore, the ultimate control mechanism needs to also deal with new tenant arrivals as well as tenant departures. We outline a conceptual design of such a mechanism in the following. To the best of our knowledge, we are not aware of any solution that provides the end-to-end solution that is needed for autonomic control in multi-tenant databases.

To allow cloud DBMSs to be self-managing, an intelligent system controller must also consider various additional aspects, specifically in the case when the database system is deployed on a pay-per-use cloud infrastructure while serving multiple application tenant instances, i.e., a multi-tenant cloud database system. In such a multi-tenant system, each tenant pays for the service provided and different tenants in the system can have competing goals. On the other hand, the service provider must share resources among the tenants, wherever possible, to minimize the operating cost to maximize profits. A controller for such a system must be able to model the dynamic characteristics and resource requirements of the different application tenants to allow elastic scaling while ensuring good tenant performance and ensuring that the tenants' service-level agreements (*SLAs*) are met. An autonomic controller consists of two logical components: the *static* component and the *dynamic* component.

The static component is responsible for modeling the behavior of the tenants and their resource usage to determine tenant placement to co-locate tenants with complementary resource requirements. The goal of this tenant placement algorithm is to minimize the total resource utilization and hence minimize operating cost while ensuring that the tenant SLAs are met. One potential approach is to use a combination of machine learning techniques to classify tenant behavior followed by tenant placement algorithms to determine optimal tenant co-location and consolidation. This model assumes that once the behavior of a tenant is modeled and a tenant placement determined, the system will continue to behave the way in which the workload was modeled, and hence is called the static component. The dynamic component complements this static model by detecting dynamic changes in the load and resource usage behavior, modeling the overall system's behavior to determine the opportune moment for elastic load balancing, selecting the minimal changes in tenant placement needed to counter the dynamic behavior, and use live database migration techniques to re-balance the tenants. In addition to modeling tenant behavior, it is also important to predict the migration cost such that a migration to minimize the operating cost does not violate a tenant's SLA. Again, we envision using machine learning models to predict the migration cost of tenants and the replacement model accounts for this cost when determining *which* tenant to migrate, *when* to migrate, and *where* to migrate [Das et al., 2010c].

6.4 DISCUSSION

As many more applications are being deployed in various cloud platforms, the need for effective means to support multi-tenancy in such architectures is also growing. In this chapter, we summarized some important aspects in the design space of multi-tenant DBMSs: the various design alternatives and abstractions for sharing in a multi-tenant DBMS, live migration techniques that are the basic primitives for supporting elasticity as a first-class feature in the database tier, and techniques for designing self-managing controllers that manage such large multi-tenant DBMS infrastructures with minimal or no human intervention.

Traditionally, DBMSs were not designed to natively support multi-tenancy. Therefore, efficiently sharing resources among independent tenant databases has posed many interesting research challenges. One fundamental question that is often asked is what performance assurances can a service provider expose to the tenants of the service. An examination of the current landscape shows that the providers only expose SLAs for availability of the service; very little is guaranteed in terms of performance. Ideally, a tenant would expect *workload-level* performance SLAs such as query throughput and/or query latency. Amazon's DynamoDB takes a first step in this direction. However, a careful study of the SLA indicates that the throughput assurance is only for the maximum supported limit. A natural question that arises is whether such a *max-only* assurance is enough to meet the application's performance goals as other tenants contend for shared resources.

From a provider's perspective, providing such workload-level performance assurances is challenging to support with high confidence, given the variety of workloads that a tenant can potentially execute. Moreover, for relational Database-as-a-Service providers, such as Microsoft SQL Azure, the problem of supporting workload-level performance SLAs is even more challenging due to the need to support arbitrary, flexible, and ad-hoc SQL queries submitted by tenant applications. For instance, when a tenant submits a new SQL query which the provider has not seen earlier, it is extremely challenging to robustly estimate the resources that will be needed to execute the query, the end-to-end wall clock time the query will take provided that resources are available, and when a query has started executing, or how much progress has it made. While the problem might be somewhat tractable for OLTP-like short transactions, a platform must also support diverse query types.

As our understanding of multi-tenant DBMSs and the various application workloads deployed in cloud infrastructures grows, it will be interesting to observe how this landscape of Database-as-a-Service matures and how the tenants of these service adapt their workloads and performance requirements in accordance with this evolving landscape.

CHAPTER 7

Concluding Remarks

During the past few years, cloud computing has emerged as a multi-billion dollar industry and as a successful paradigm for web application deployment. Irrespective of the cloud provider or the cloud abstraction, data are central to applications deployed in the cloud. Since DBMSs store and serve an application's critical data, they form a mission-critical component in the cloud software stack. DBMSs deployed in a cloud infrastructure and supporting diverse applications face unique challenges. The overarching goal of the current research and development efforts is to enable DBMSs to scale-out while efficiently supporting transactional semantics and being elastic without introducing high performance overhead. On one hand, the ability to scale-out using clusters of commodity servers allows the DBMSs to leverage from the economies of scale, and the ability to efficiently support transactional semantics simplifies application design. On the other hand, the ability to dynamically scale-up and scale-down the number of nodes in a live DBMS allows the system to consolidate to fewer nodes during periods of low load and to add nodes when the load increases. This elastic scaling leverages the underlying pay-per-use cloud infrastructure to minimize the system's operating cost and ensures good performance.

This book summarizes the current state-of-the-art in the two thrust areas of scale-out transaction processing and lightweight elasticity. In the context of scale-out transaction processing, we reviewed the design and implementation of several systems that strive to provide transactions access to the underlying data by deploying a range of classical techniques borrowed from the areas of distributed computing and database transaction processing. In the context of lightweight elasticity in DBMSs, we reviewed the design and implementation of recently proposed techniques for live data migration for different types of database architectures. We would like to point out that the general area of scalable data-management in the cloud is evolving relatively rapidly. For example, recently both Google and Facebook have announced new data-management architectures and systems for transactional consistency over data stored in the cloud. In particular, Google recently developed a system called Spanner [Corbett et al., 2012] for managing transactional data in a multi-cloud environment. Similarly, Facebook has recently presented a system called Tao [Venkataramani et al., 2012], which is one of the few systems that uses the operational semantics of application-level transactions to ensure transactional atomicity in NoSQL data-stores. Understanding of scale-out transaction processing and light-weight elasticity of databases is critical for the design of next-generation DBMSs for cloud computing infrastructures.

In traditional enterprise settings, transaction processing and data analysis systems are typically managed as separate systems. The rationale behind this separation is that OLTP and analysis workloads have very different characteristics and requirements. Therefore, in terms of performance, it is prudent to separate the two types of systems [Stonebraker et al., 2007]. However, the growing need for real-time analysis and the costs involved in managing two different systems have resulted in the compelling need for the convergence of the transaction processing and data analysis systems, especially in cloud infrastructures. In this book, we focused on the design of OLTP systems and presented the design principles and architectures for such systems. One major challenge in the design of these hybrid systems is to find the suitable design principles and architectures that will allow scale-out, elasticity, and augmented functionality. A thorough analysis of the design space and the candidate systems is essential in distilling the design principles of the on-line transaction and analytical processing (OLTAP) systems.

The current cloud infrastructure consists of a static collection of powerful data centers (or cores). This model misses out on the substantial computing power that resides outside the data centers. We envision a dynamic cloud that will be formed of the static cloud that forms the nucleus of the infrastructure and a collection of cores that dynamically join the cloud from time to time. Such an infrastructure presents challenges beyond the current generation of cloud infrastructures. Examples of some challenges are: How to provide a consistent and uniform namespace spanning the dynamic collection of cloud cores? What are the practical consistency models and abstractions for such large-scale dynamic environments? How to efficiently integrate surplus capacity as and when they become available? How to effectively migrate load and data and efficiently replicate state across the cores? And how to monitor and model such large-scale systems? Extending the designs of elastic, self-managing, and scalable systems to this dynamic cloud infrastructure spanning larger scale operations, higher network latency, and lower network bandwidth is a worthwhile direction for future work.

Bibliography

Divyakant Agrawal, Amr El Abbadi, Shyam Antony, and Sudipto Das. Data Management Challenges in Cloud Computing Infrastructures. In *6th Int. Workshop on Databases in Networked Information Systems*, pages 1–10, 2010. DOI: 10.1007/978-3-642-12038-1_1 Cited on page(s) 5

Marcos K. Aguilera, Arif Merchant, Mehul Shah, Alistair Veitch, and Christos Karamanolis. Sinfonia: a new paradigm for building scalable distributed systems. In *Proc. 21st ACM Symp. on Operating System Principles*, pages 159–174, 2007. DOI: 10.1145/1323293.1294278 Cited on page(s) 79, 81

Apache Hadoop. The Apache Hadoop Project. http://hadoop.apache.org/, 20012. Retrieved October 1, 2012. Cited on page(s) 4

Stefan Aulbach, Torsten Grust, Dean Jacobs, Alfons Kemper, and Jan Rittinger. Multi-tenant databases for software as a service: schema-mapping techniques. In *Proc. ACM SIGMOD Int. Conf. on Management of Data*, pages 1195–1206, 2008. DOI: 10.1145/1376616.1376736 Cited on page(s) 86

Jason Baker, Chris Bond, James Corbett, JJ Furman, Andrey Khorlin, James Larson, Jean-Michel Leon, Yawei Li, Alexander Lloyd, and Vadim Yushprakh. Megastore: Providing Scalable, Highly Available Storage for Interactive Services. In *Proc. 5th Biennial Conf. on Innovative Data Systems Research*, pages 223–234, 2011. Cited on page(s) 42, 60

Mahesh Balakrishnan, Dahlia Malkhi, Vijayan Prabhakaran, and Ted Wobber. CORFU: A Shared Log Design for Flash Clusters. In *Proc. 9th USENIX Symp. on Networked Systems Design & Implementation*, 2012. Cited on page(s) 67

Sean Barker, Yun Chi, Hyun Jin Moon, Hakan Hacigümüş, and Prashant Shenoy. "cut me some slack": latency-aware live migration for databases. In *Proc. 15th Int. Conf. on Extending Database Technology*, pages 432–443, 2012. DOI: 10.1145/2247596.2247647 Cited on page(s) 98, 100

Hal Berenson, Phil Bernstein, Jim Gray, Jim Melton, Elizabeth O'Neil, and Patrick O'Neil. A critique of ANSI SQL isolation levels. In *Proc. ACM SIGMOD Int. Conf. on Management of Data*, pages 1–10, 1995. DOI: 10.1145/568271.223785 Cited on page(s) 51, 77

P. A. Bernstein, V. Hadzilacos, and N. Goodman. *Concurrency Control and Recovery in Database Systems*. Addison Wesley, Reading, Massachusetts, 1987. Cited on page(s) 18

108 BIBLIOGRAPHY

Philip Bernstein, Colin Reid, and Sudipto Das. Hyder - A Transactional Record Manager for Shared Flash. In *Proc. 5th Biennial Conf. on Innovative Data Systems Research*, pages 9–20, 2011a. Cited on page(s) 48, 65

Philip A. Bernstein and Eric Newcomer. *Principles of Transaction Processing*. Morgan-Kaufmann Publishers Inc., second edition, 2009. Cited on page(s) 22, 57, 90

Philip A. Bernstein, Istvan Cseri, Nishant Dani, Nigel Ellis, Ajay Kalhan, Gopal Kakivaya, David B. Lomet, Ramesh Manner, Lev Novik, and Tomas Talius. Adapting Microsoft SQL Server for Cloud Computing. In *Proc. 27th Int. Conf. on Data Engineering*, pages 1255–1263, 2011b. DOI: 10.1109/ICDE.2011.5767935 Cited on page(s) 43, 58, 60

Philip A. Bernstein, Colin W. Reid, Ming Wu, and Xinhao Yuan. Optimistic concurrency control by melding trees. *Proc. VLDB Endowment*, 4(11):944–955, 2011c. Cited on page(s) 67

Kenneth P. Birman. Replication and fault-tolerance in the isis system. In *Proc. 10th ACM Symp. on Operating System Principles*, pages 79–86, 1985. DOI: 10.1145/323647.323636 Cited on page(s) 14, 15

Peter Bodík, Moisés Goldszmidt, and Armando Fox. Hilighter: Automatically building robust signatures of performance behavior for small- and large-scale systems. In *Third Workshop on Tackling Computer Systems Problems with Machine Learning Techniques*, pages 1–6, 2008. Cited on page(s) 100

Matthias Brantner, Daniela Florescu, David Graf, Donald Kossmann, and Tim Kraska. Building a database on S3. In *Proc. ACM SIGMOD Int. Conf. on Management of Data*, pages 251–264, 2008. DOI: 10.1145/1376616.1376645 Cited on page(s) 71, 73, 81

Eric A. Brewer. Towards robust distributed systems (Invited Talk). In *Proc. ACM SIGACT-SIGOPS 19th Symp. on the Principles of Distributed Computing*, page 7, 2000. Cited on page(s) 16

Eric A. Brewer. Pushing the cap: Strategies for consistency and availability. *IEEE Computer*, 45(2):23–29, 2012. DOI: 10.1109/MC.2012.37 Cited on page(s) 16

Mike Burrows. The Chubby Lock Service for Loosely-Coupled Distributed Systems. In *Proc. 7th USENIX Symp. on Operating System Design and Implementation*, pages 335–350, 2006. Cited on page(s) 26, 63

Bengt Carlsson and Rune Gustavsson. The rise and fall of napster - an evolutionary approach. In *Proc. of the 6th Int. Computer Science Conf. on Active Media Technology*, pages 347–354, 2001. DOI: 10.1007/3-540-45336-9_40 Cited on page(s) 17

Rick Cattell. Scalable SQL and NoSQL data stores. *SIGMOD Rec.*, 39(4):12–27, December 2011. DOI: 10.1145/1978915.1978919 Cited on page(s) 37

Tushar D. Chandra, Robert Griesemer, and Joshua Redstone. Paxos made live: an engineering perspective. In *Proc. ACM SIGACT-SIGOPS 26th Symp. on the Principles of Distributed Computing*, pages 398–407, 2007. DOI: 10.1145/1281100.1281103 Cited on page(s) 26, 61

Ernest Chang and Rosemary Roberts. An improved algorithm for decentralized extrema-finding in circular configurations of processes. *Commun. ACM*, 22(5):281–283, May 1979. DOI: 10.1145/359104.359108 Cited on page(s) 12

Fay Chang, Jeffrey Dean, Sanjay Ghemawat, Wilson C. Hsieh, Deborah A. Wallach, Mike Burrows, Tushar Chandra, Andrew Fikes, and Robert E. Gruber. Bigtable: A Distributed Storage System for Structured Data. In *Proc. 7th USENIX Symp. on Operating System Design and Implementation*, pages 205–218, 2006. Cited on page(s) 4, 25, 31, 32

Navraj Chohan, Chris Bunch, Sydney Pang, Chandra Krintz, Nagy Mostafa, Sunil Soman, and Richard Wolski. Appscale: Scalable and open appengine application development and deployment. In *Proc. of 1st Int. Conf. on Cloud Computing*, pages 57–70, 2009. Cited on page(s) 88

Christopher Clark, Keir Fraser, Steven Hand, Jacob Gorm Hansen, Eric Jul, Christian Limpach, Ian Pratt, and Andrew Warfield. Live migration of virtual machines. In *Proc. 2nd USENIX Symp. on Networked Systems Design & Implementation*, pages 273–286, 2005. Cited on page(s) 88, 100

Brian F. Cooper, Raghu Ramakrishnan, Utkarsh Srivastava, Adam Silberstein, Philip Bohannon, Hans-Arno Jacobsen, Nick Puz, Daniel Weaver, and Ramana Yerneni. PNUTS: Yahoo!'s hosted data serving platform. *Proc. VLDB Endowment*, 1(2):1277–1288, 2008. Cited on page(s) 4, 25, 26, 33

Brian F. Cooper, Adam Silberstein, Erwin Tam, Raghu Ramakrishnan, and Russell Sears. Benchmarking Cloud Serving Systems with YCSB. In *Proc. 1st ACM Symp. on Cloud Computing*, pages 143–154, 2010. DOI: 10.1145/1807128.1807152 Cited on page(s) 27, 37

James C. Corbett, Jeffrey Dean, Michael Epstein, Andrew Fikes, Christopher Frost, JJ Furman, Sanjay Ghemawat, Andrey Gubarev, Christopher Heiser, Peter Hochschild, Wilson Hsieh, Sebastian Kanthak, Eugene Kogan, Hongyi Li, Alexander Lloyd, Sergey Melnik, David Mwaura, David Nagle, Sean Quinlan, Rajesh Rao, Lindsay Rolig, Yasushi Saito, Michal Szymaniak, Christopher Taylor, Ruth Wang, and Dale Woodford. Spanner: Google's Globally-Distributed Database. In *Proc. 10th USENIX Symp. on Operating System Design and Implementation*, pages 251–264, 2012. Cited on page(s) 82, 105

Carlo Curino, Yang Zhang, Evan P. C. Jones, and Samuel Madden. Schism: a workload-driven approach to database replication and partitioning. *Proc. VLDB Endowment*, 3(1):48–57, 2010. Cited on page(s) 44, 45, 64

Carlo Curino, Evan Jones, Raluca Popa, Nirmesh Malviya, Eugene Wu, Sam Madden, Hari Balakrishnan, and Nickolai Zeldovich. Relational Cloud: A Database Service for the Cloud. In *Proc.*

5th Biennial Conf. on Innovative Data Systems Research, pages 235–240, 2011a. Cited on page(s) 64, 99

Carlo Curino, Evan P. C. Jones, Samuel Madden, and Hari Balakrishnan. Workload-aware database monitoring and consolidation. In *Proc. ACM SIGMOD Int. Conf. on Management of Data*, pages 313–324, 2011b. DOI: 10.1145/1989323.1989357 Cited on page(s) 65, 84, 85, 86, 102

Danga Interactive Inc. Memcached: A distributed memory object caching system. http://www.danga.com/memcached/, 2012. Retrieved: November 2012. Cited on page(s) 37

Sudipto Das. *Scalable and Elastic Transactional Data Stores for Cloud Computing Platforms*. PhD thesis, UC Santa Barbara, December 2011. Cited on page(s) 55, 58, 92

Sudipto Das, Divyakant Agrawal, and Amr El Abbadi. ElasTraS: An Elastic Transactional Data Store in the Cloud. In *1st. USENIX Workshop on Hot topics on Cloud Computing*, pages 1–5, 2009. Cited on page(s) 56

Sudipto Das, Shashank Agarwal, Divyakant Agrawal, and Amr El Abbadi. ElasTraS: An Elastic, Scalable, and Self Managing Transactional Database for the Cloud. Technical Report 2010-04, Computer Science, University of California Santa Barbara, 2010a. Cited on page(s) 41, 56

Sudipto Das, Divyakant Agrawal, and Amr El Abbadi. G-Store: A Scalable Data Store for Transactional Multi key Access in the Cloud. In *Proc. 1st ACM Symp. on Cloud Computing*, pages 163–174, 2010b. DOI: 10.1145/1807128.1807157 Cited on page(s) 46, 47, 52

Sudipto Das, Shoji Nishimura, Divyakant Agrawal, and Amr El Abbadi. Live Database Migration for Elasticity in a Multitenant Database for Cloud Platforms. Technical Report 2010-09, Computer Science, University of California Santa Barbara, 2010c. Cited on page(s) 104

Sudipto Das, Shoji Nishimura, Divyakant Agrawal, and Amr El Abbadi. Albatross: Lightweight Elasticity in Shared Storage Databases for the Cloud using Live Data Migration. *Proc. VLDB Endowment*, 4(8):494–505, May 2011. Cited on page(s) 58

Jeff Dean. Talk at the Google Faculty Summit, 2010. Cited on page(s) 5

Jeffrey Dean and Sanjay Ghemawat. MapReduce: simplified data processing on large clusters. In *OSDI*, pages 137–150, 2004. DOI: 10.1145/1327452.1327492 Cited on page(s) 4

Jeffrey Dean and Sanjay Ghemawat. Mapreduce: a flexible data processing tool. *Commun. CACM*, 53(1):72–77, 2010. DOI: 10.1145/1629175.1629198 Cited on page(s) 4

Giuseppe DeCandia, Deniz Hastorun, Madan Jampani, Gunavardhan Kakulapati, Avinash Lakshman, Alex Pilchin, Swaminathan Sivasubramanian, Peter Vosshall, and Werner Vogels. Dynamo: Amazon's highly available key-value store. In *Proc. 21st ACM Symp. on Operating System Principles*, pages 205–220, 2007. DOI: 10.1145/1323293.1294281 Cited on page(s) 4, 25, 26, 35

Xavier Défago, André Schiper, and Péter Urbán. Total order broadcast and multicast algorithms: Taxonomy and survey. *ACM Comput. Surv.*, 36(4):372–421, 2004. DOI: 10.1145/1041680.1041682 Cited on page(s) 15

Danny Dolev.   The byzantine generals strike again.   *J. Algorithms*, 3(1):14–30, 1982. DOI: 10.1016/0196-6774(82)90004-9 Cited on page(s) 16

DRS. Resource management with VMware DRS. `http://vmware.com/pdf/vmware_drs_wp.pdf`, 2006. Retrieved: November 2012. Cited on page(s) 100

Songyun Duan, Vamsidhar Thummala, and Shivnath Babu. Tuning database configuration parameters with ituned. *Proc. VLDB Endow.*, 2:1246–1257, August 2009. Cited on page(s) 100

Aaron J. Elmore, Sudipto Das, Divyakant Agrawal, and Amr El Abbadi. Zephyr: Live Migration in Shared Nothing Databases for Elastic Cloud Platforms. In *Proc. ACM SIGMOD Int. Conf. on Management of Data*, pages 301–312, 2011. DOI: 10.1145/1989323.1989356 Cited on page(s) 97, 98

K. P. Eswaran, J. N. Gray, R. A. Lorie, and I. L. Traiger. The notions of consistency and predicate locks in a database system. *Commun. ACM*, 19(11):624–633, 1976. DOI: 10.1145/360363.360369 Cited on page(s) 5, 20, 48

Michael J. Fischer, Nancy A. Lynch, and Mike Paterson. Impossibility of distributed consensus with one faulty process. In *Proc. 2nd ACM SIGACT-SIGMOD Symp. on Principles of Database Systems*, pages 1–7, 1983. DOI: 10.1145/588058.588060 Cited on page(s) 16, 17

Michael J. Fischer, Nancy A. Lynch, and Mike Paterson. Impossibility of distributed consensus with one faulty process. *J. ACM*, 32(2):374–382, 1985. DOI: 10.1145/3149.214121 Cited on page(s) 16

H. Garcia-Molina. Elections in a distributed computing system. *IEEE Trans. Comput.*, 31(1):48–59, January 1982. DOI: 10.1109/TC.1982.1675885 Cited on page(s) 12

Sanjay Ghemawat, Howard Gobioff, and Shun-Tak Leung. The Google file system. In *Proc. 19th ACM Symp. on Operating System Principles*, pages 29–43, 2003. DOI: 10.1145/945445.945450 Cited on page(s) 26, 49

David K. Gifford. Weighted voting for replicated data. In *Proc. 7th ACM Symp. on Operating System Principles*, pages 150–162, 1979. DOI: 10.1145/800215.806583 Cited on page(s) 11

Seth Gilbert and Nancy Lynch.   Brewer's conjecture and the feasibility of consistent, available, partition-tolerant web services.   *SIGACT News*, 33(2):51–59, 2002. DOI: 10.1145/564585.564601 Cited on page(s) 16

Seth Gilbert and Nancy A. Lynch. Perspectives on the CAP Theorem. *IEEE Computer*, 45(2): 30–36, 2012. DOI: 10.1109/MC.2011.389 Cited on page(s) 17

Olivier Goldschmidt and Dorit S. Hochbaum. Polynomial algorithm for the k-cut problem. In *Proc. 29th Annual Symp. on Foundations of Computer Science*, pages 444–451, 1988. DOI: 10.1109/SFCS.1988.21960 Cited on page(s) 45

Google Protocol Buffers. Google protocol buffers. `http://code.google.com/apis/protocolbuffers/`, 2012. Retrieved: November 2012. Cited on page(s) 99

Jim Gray. Notes on data base operating systems. In *Operating Systems, An Advanced Course*, pages 393–481. Springer-Verlag, 1978. DOI: 10.1007/3-540-08755-9_9 Cited on page(s) 5, 22, 63

Jim Gray and Andreas Reuter. *Transaction Processing: Concepts and Techniques*. Morgan Kaufmann Publishers Inc., 1992. Cited on page(s) 7, 22

A. Gulati, C. Kumar, I. Ahamad, and K. Kumar. BASIL: Automated IO load balancing across storage devices. In *Proc. 8th USENIX Conf. on File and Storage Technologies*, 2010. Cited on page(s) 101

A. Gulati, G. Shanmugathan, I. Ahamad, C. waldspurger, and M. Uysal. Pesto: Online Storage Perfromance Management in Virtualized Datacenters. In *Proc. 2nd ACM Symp. on Cloud Computing*, 2011. DOI: 10.1145/2038916.2038935 Cited on page(s) 102

Hakan Hacigümüs, Jun'ichi Tatemura, Wang-Pin Hsiung, Hyun Jin Moon, Oliver Po, Arsany Sawires, Yun Chi, and Hojjat Jafarpour. CloudDB: One Size Fits All Revived. In *6th World Congress on Services*, pages 148–149, 2010. DOI: 10.1109/SERVICES.2010.96 Cited on page(s) 98

James Hamilton. I love eventual consistency but... `http://bit.ly/hamilton-eventual`, April 2010. Retrieved: October 2011. Cited on page(s) 5, 39

hbase. HBase: Bigtable-like structured storage for Hadoop HDFS. `http://hbase.apache.org/`, 2011. Retrieved: October 2011. Cited on page(s)

HDFS. HDFS: A distributed file system that provides high throughput access to application data. `http://hadoop.apache.org/hdfs/`, 2011. Retrieved: October 2011. Cited on page(s) 56

Pat Helland. Life beyond Distributed Transactions: An Apostate's Opinion. In *Proc. 3rd Biennial Conf. on Innovative Data Systems Research*, pages 132–141, 2007. Cited on page(s) 27

Dean Jacobs and Stefan Aulbach. Ruminations on multi-tenant databases. In *Proc. Datenbanksysteme in Business, Technologie und Web*, pages 514–521, 2007. Cited on page(s) 83, 84

M. Frans Kaashoek, Andrew S. Tanenbaum, Susan Flynn Hummel, and Henri E. Bal. An efficient reliable broadcast protocol. *Operating Systems Review*, 23(4):5–19, 1989. DOI: 10.1145/70730.70732 Cited on page(s) 15

Robert Kallman, Hideaki Kimura, Jonathan Natkins, Andrew Pavlo, Alex Rasin, Stanley B. Zdonik, Evan P. C. Jones, Samuel Madden, Michael Stonebraker, Yang Zhang, John Hugg, and Daniel J. Abadi. H-store: a high-performance, distributed main memory transaction processing system. *Proc. VLDB Endowment*, 1(2):1496–1499, 2008. Cited on page(s) 41

David Karger, Eric Lehman, Tom Leighton, Rina Panigrahy, Matthew Levine, and Daniel Lewin. Consistent hashing and random trees: distributed caching protocols for relieving hot spots on the world wide web. In *Proc. 29th Annual ACM Symp. on Theory of Computing*, pages 654–663, 1997. DOI: 10.1145/258533.258660 Cited on page(s) 35

Tim Kraska, Martin Hentschel, Gustavo Alonso, and Donald Kossmann. Consistency Rationing in the Cloud: Pay only when it matters. *Proc. VLDB Endowment*, 2(1):253–264, 2009. Cited on page(s) 74, 75

H. T. Kung and John T. Robinson. On optimistic methods for concurrency control. *ACM Trans. Database Syst.*, 6(2):213–226, 1981. DOI: 10.1145/319566.319567 Cited on page(s) 21

Leslie Lamport. Time, clocks, and the ordering of events in a distributed system. *Commun. ACM*, 21(7):558–565, 1978. DOI: 10.1145/359545.359563 Cited on page(s) 8, 11, 26

Leslie Lamport. The part-time parliament. *ACM Trans. Comp. Syst.*, 16(2):133–169, 1998. DOI: 10.1145/279227.279229 Cited on page(s) 16, 26, 61

Leslie Lamport. Paxos made simple. *SIGACT News*, 32(4):18–25, Dec. 2001. DOI: 10.1145/568425.568433 Cited on page(s) 16

Justin J. Levandoski, David B. Lomet, Mohamed F. Mokbel, and Kevin Zhao. Deuteronomy: Transaction support for cloud data. In *Proc. 5th Biennial Conf. on Innovative Data Systems Research*, pages 123–133, 2011. Cited on page(s) 48, 68

Wyatt Lloyd, Michael J. Freedman, Michael Kaminsky, and David G. Andersen. Don't settle for eventual: scalable causal consistency for wide-area storage with COPS. In *Proc. 23rd ACM Symp. on Operating System Principles*, pages 401–416, 2011. DOI: 10.1145/2043556.2043593 Cited on page(s) 82

David B. Lomet and Mohamed F. Mokbel. Locking Key Ranges with Unbundled Transaction Services. *PVLDB*, 2(1):265–276, 2009. Cited on page(s) 69

David B. Lomet, Alan Fekete, Gerhard Weikum, and Michael J. Zwilling. Unbundling transaction services in the cloud. In *Proc. 4th Biennial Conf. on Innovative Data Systems Research*, 2009. Cited on page(s) 68

Mamoru Maekawa. A square root n algorithm for mutual exclusion in decentralized systems. *ACM Trans. Comput. Syst.*, 3(2):145–159, 1985. DOI: 10.1145/214438.214445 Cited on page(s) 11

Keith Marzullo and Susan Owicki. Maintaining the time in a distributed system. In *Proc. ACM SIGACT-SIGOPS 2nd Symp. on the Principles of Distributed Computing*, pages 295–305, 1983. DOI: 10.1145/800221.806730 Cited on page(s) 82

C. Mohan, Don Haderle, Bruce Lindsay, Hamid Pirahesh, and Peter Schwarz. Aries: a transaction recovery method supporting fine-granularity locking and partial rollbacks using write-ahead logging. *ACM Trans. Database Syst.*, 17(1):94–162, 1992. DOI: 10.1145/128765.128770 Cited on page(s) 48, 97

Vivek Narasayya, Sudipto Das, Manoj Syamala, Badrish Chandramouli, and Surajit Chaudhuri. SQLVM: Performance Isolation in Multi-Tenant Relational Database-as-a-Service. In *Proc. 6th Biennial Conf. on Innovative Data Systems Research*, pages 1–9, 2013. Cited on page(s) 86

Simo Neuvonen, Antoni Wolski, Markku manner, and Vilho Raatikka. Telecommunication application transaction processing (tatp) benchmark description 1.0. http://tatpbenchmark.sourceforge.net/TATP_Description.pdf, March 2009. Retrieved: October 2011. Cited on page(s) 41

NoSQL. The NoSQL Movement. http://en.wikipedia.org/wiki/NoSQL, 2012. Accessed: October 1, 2012. Cited on page(s) 5

Dare Obasanjo. When databases lie: Consistency vs. availability in distributed systems. http://bit.ly/obasanjo_CAP, October 2009. Retrieved: October 2011. Cited on page(s) 5, 39

Diego Ongaro, Stephen M. Rumble, Ryan Stutsman, John K. Ousterhout, and Mendel Rosenblum. Fast crash recovery in ramcloud. In *Proc. 23rd ACM Symp. on Operating System Principles*, pages 29–41, 2011. DOI: 10.1145/2043556.2043560 Cited on page(s) 37

John K. Ousterhout, Parag Agrawal, David Erickson, Christos Kozyrakis, Jacob Leverich, David Mazières, Subhasish Mitra, Aravind Narayanan, Guru M. Parulkar, Mendel Rosenblum, Stephen M. Rumble, Eric Stratmann, and Ryan Stutsman. The case for ramclouds: scalable high-performance storage entirely in dram. *Operating Systems Review*, 43(4):92–105, 2009. DOI: 10.1145/1713254.1713276 Cited on page(s) 37

M. Tamer Özsu and Patrick Valduriez. *Principles of Distributed Database Systems*. Springer, 3rd edition, 2011. DOI: 10.1007/978-1-4419-8834-8 Cited on page(s) 5, 7

Christos H. Papadimitriou. The serializability of concurrent database updates. *J. ACM*, 26(4):631–653, October 1979. DOI: 10.1145/322154.322158 Cited on page(s) 20

Stacy Patterson, Aaron J. Elmore, Faisal Nawab, Divyakant Agrawal, and Amr El Abbadi. Serializability, not serial: Concurrency control and availability in multi-datacenter datastores. *Proc. VLDB Endowment*, 5(11):1459–1470, 2012. Cited on page(s) 63

Marshall C. Pease, Robert E. Shostak, and Leslie Lamport. Reaching agreement in the presence of faults. *J. ACM*, 27(2):228–234, 1980. DOI: 10.1145/322186.322188 Cited on page(s) 15

Daniel Peng and Frank Dabek. Large-scale incremental processing using distributed transactions and notifications. In *Proc. 9th USENIX Symp. on Operating System Design and Implementation*, 2010. Cited on page(s) 77, 79

Percona. Percona XtraBackup. `http://www.percona.com/software/percona-xtrabackup/`, 2012. Retrieved: November 2012. Cited on page(s) 100

Colin W. Reid and Philip A. Bernstein. Implementing an append-only interface for semiconductor storage. *IEEE Data Eng. Bull.*, 33(4):14–20, 2010. Cited on page(s) 67

Berthold Reinwald. Database support for multi-tenant applications. In *IEEE Workshop on Information and Software as Services*, 2010. Cited on page(s) 83, 87

Marc Shapiro, Nuno Preguiça, Carlos Baquero, and Marek Zawirski. Conflict-free replicated data types. In *Proc. of the 13th Int. Conf. on Stabilization, Safety, and Security of Distributed Systems*, pages 386–400, 2011. DOI: 10.1007/978-3-642-24550-3_29 Cited on page(s) 77

Jeff Shute, Mircea Oancea, Stephan Ellner, Ben Handy, Eric Rollins, Bart Samwel, Radek Vingralek, Chad Whipkey, Xin Chen, Beat Jegerlehner, Kyle Littlefield, and Phoenix Tong. F1: the fault-tolerant distributed RDBMS supporting Google's ad business. In *Proc. ACM SIGMOD Int. Conf. on Management of Data*, pages 777–778, 2012. DOI: 10.1145/2213836.2213954 Cited on page(s) 82

D. Skeen and M. Stonebraker. A formal model of crash recovery in a distributed system. *IEEE Trans. Softw. Eng.*, 9(3):219–228, 1983. DOI: 10.1109/TSE.1983.236608 Cited on page(s) 23

Ahmed A. Soror, Umar Farooq Minhas, Ashraf Aboulnaga, Kenneth Salem, Peter Kokosielis, and Sunil Kamath. Automatic virtual machine configuration for database workloads. In *Proc. ACM SIGMOD Int. Conf. on Management of Data*, pages 953–966, 2008. DOI: 10.1145/1670243.1670250 Cited on page(s) 84

Yair Sovran, Russell Power, Marcos K. Aguilera, and Jinyang Li. Transactional storage for geo-replicated systems. In *Proc. 23rd ACM Symp. on Operating System Principles*, pages 385–400, 2011. DOI: 10.1145/2043556.2043592 Cited on page(s) 75, 76, 77

Ion Stoica, Robert Morris, David Karger, M. Frans Kaashoek, and Hari Balakrishnan. Chord: A scalable peer-to-peer lookup service for internet applications. In *SIGCOMM*, pages 149–160, 2001. DOI: 10.1145/964723.383071 Cited on page(s) 17, 26, 28, 35

Michael Stonebraker, Chuck Bear, Ugur Cetintemel, Mitch Cherniack, Tingjian Ge, Nabil Hachem, Stavros Harizopoulos, John Lifter, and Jennie Rogersand Stanley B. Zdonik. One Size Fits All? Part 2: Benchmarking Studies. In *Proc. 3rd Biennial Conf. on Innovative Data Systems Research*, pages 173–184, 2007. Cited on page(s) 106

Michael Stonebraker, Daniel J. Abadi, David J. DeWitt, Samuel Madden, Erik Paulson, Andrew Pavlo, and Alexander Rasin. Mapreduce and parallel dbmss: friends or foes? *Commun. CACM*, 53(1):64–71, 2010. Cited on page(s) 4

Junichi Tatemura, Oliver Po, and Hakan Hacgümüş. Microsharding: a declarative approach to support elastic OLTP workloads. *SIGOPS Oper. Syst. Rev.*, 46(1):4–11, 2012. DOI: 10.1145/2146382.2146385 Cited on page(s) 98

Alexander Thomson, Thaddeus Diamond, Shu-Chun Weng, Kun Ren, Philip Shao, and Daniel J. Abadi. Calvin: fast distributed transactions for partitioned database systems. In *Proc. ACM SIGMOD Int. Conf. on Management of Data*, pages 1–12, 2012. DOI: 10.1145/2213836.2213838 Cited on page(s) 81

TPC-C. TPC-C benchmark (Version 5.11), February 2010. Retrieved: October 2011. Cited on page(s) 41

Bhuvan Urgaonkar, Arnold L. Rosenberg, and Prashant J. Shenoy. Application placement on a cluster of servers. *Int. J. Found. Comput. Sci.*, 18(5):1023–1041, 2007. DOI: 10.1142/S012905410700511X Cited on page(s) 100

Venkateshwaran Venkataramani, Zach Amsden, Nathan Bronson, George Cabrera III, Prasad Chakka, Peter Dimov, Hui Ding, Jack Ferris, Anthony Giardullo, Jeremy Hoon, Sachin Kulkarni, Nathan Lawrence, Mark Marchukov, Dmitri Petrov, and Lovro Puzar. Tao: how facebook serves the social graph. In *Proc. ACM SIGMOD Int. Conf. on Management of Data*, pages 791–792, 2012. DOI: 10.1145/2213836.2213957 Cited on page(s) 105

Hoang Tam Vo, Chun Chen, and Beng Chin Ooi. Towards elastic transactional cloud storage with range query support. *Proc. VLDB Endowment*, 3(1):506–517, 2010. Cited on page(s) 81

Werner Vogels. Data access patterns in the amazon.com technology platform. In *Proc. 33rd Int. Conf. on Very Large Data Bases*, pages 1–1, 2007. Cited on page(s) 25

Werner Vogels. Eventually consistent. *Commun. ACM*, 52(1):40–44, 2009. ISSN 0001-0782. DOI: 10.1145/1435417.1435432 Cited on page(s) 26

Gerhard Weikum and Gottfried Vossen. *Transactional information systems: theory, algorithms, and the practice of concurrency control and recovery*. Morgan Kaufmann Publishers Inc., 2001. Cited on page(s) 7, 22, 48, 57

Gerhard Weikum, Axel Moenkeberg, Christof Hasse, and Peter Zabback. Self-tuning database technology and information services: from wishful thinking to viable engineering. In *Proc. 28th Int. Conf. on Very Large Data Bases*, pages 20–31, 2002. Cited on page(s) 100

Craig D. Weissman and Steve Bobrowski. The design of the force.com multitenant internet application development platform. In *Proc. ACM SIGMOD Int. Conf. on Management of Data*, pages 889–896, 2009. DOI: 10.1145/1559845.1559942 Cited on page(s) 83, 86

Pengcheng Xiong, Yun Chi, Shenghuo Zhu, Hyun Jin Moon, Calton Pu, and Hakan Hacigumus. Intelligent management of virtualized resources for database systems in cloud environment. In *Proc. 27th Int. Conf. on Data Engineering*, pages 87–98, 2011. DOI: 10.1109/ICDE.2011.5767928 Cited on page(s) 84

Authors' Biographies

DIVYAKANT AGRAWAL

Divyakant Agrawal is a Professor of Computer Science in the Department of Computer Science at the University of California at Santa Barbara. His research expertise is in the areas of database systems, distributed computing, data warehousing, and large-scale information systems. He is a Fellow of the ACM and the IEEE. He has published more than 300 articles in the fields of database systems, distributed systems, multi-dimensional indexing, data warehousing, and cloud data management. He has served on numerous program committees of international conferences, symposia, and workshops and served as an editor of the *Journal of Distributed and Parallel Databases* from 1993–2008 and *the VLDB Journal* from 2003–2008. He was the program chair of ACM SIGMOD 2010 and has served as the general chair for multiple ACM SIGSPATIAL conferences. He is currently serving as the editor-in-chief of the *Journal of Distributed and Parallel Databases* and on the editorial boards of ACM TODS and IEEE TKDE. He is also serving as a Trustee on the VLDB endowment. He has been on the faculty of UC Santa Barbara for more than 25 years and has graduated more than 30 Ph.D. students. He is also the recipient of the UCSB Outstanding Graduate Mentor Award.

SUDIPTO DAS

Sudipto Das is currently a Researcher in the eXtreme Computing Group (XCG) at Microsoft Research (MSR). Dr. Das received his Ph.D. in Computer Science from University of California Santa Barbara (UCSB). His research interests lie in the broad area of scalable data management systems and distributed systems. His research spans multiple areas such as scalable transaction processing systems for cloud computing platforms, advanced data analysis systems for big data, and multi-tenant database systems. His works have been published in various prestigious and highly selective venues showcasing database research, such as SIGMOD, VLDB, ICDE, CIDR, MDM, and SoCC. He has also delivered several tutorials in the area of big data and cloud computing. Dr. Das is the recipient of UCSB's 2012 Lancaster Dissertation award, the CIDR 2011 Best Paper Award, MDM 2011 Best Runner-up Paper Award, the 2012 Outstanding Dissertation Award, and the 2011 Outstanding Student Award in Computer Science at UC Santa Barbara, and the TCS-JU Best Student Award for 2006.

AMR EL ABBADI

Amr El Abbadi is currently a Professor in the Computer Science Department at the University of California, Santa Barbara (UCSB). He received his B. Eng. in Computer Science from Alexandria University, Egypt, and received his M.S. and Ph.D. in Computer Science from Cornell University. He chaired the Computer Science Department at UCSB from 2007–2011. Prof. El Abbadi is a Fellow of the ACM and AAAS. He has served as a journal editor for several database journals, including, currently, *The VLDB Journal*. He has been Program Chair for multiple database and distributed systems conferences, including VLDB 2000, SIGSPATIAL GIS 2010, and ACM Symposium on Cloud Computing (SoCC) 2011. He has also served as a board member of the VLDB Endowment from 2002–2008. In 2007, Prof. El Abbadi received the UCSB Senate Outstanding Mentorship Award for his excellence in mentoring graduate students. He has published over 275 articles in databases and distributed systems.

Printed in the United States
by Baker & Taylor Publisher Services